THE YOUNG

ENTREPRENEUR

By Robert Farias

Entrepreneur: Originates from the French term for a person who organizes and manages any enterprise, esp. a business, usually with considerable initiative and risk.

Have you ever caught yourself asking these questions: "Why am I here on earth? What is my purpose in life? What type of career and lifestyle do I plan on having?" This book will serve as a guide for answering these questions, by showing you that you are in control of your own destiny!

THE FIVE BASIC QUESTIONS YOU SHOULD ASK YOURSELF:

What are my good qualities and talents?

_____

What career do I want?

_____

How long will it take me to achieve this career?

_____

Will I enjoy the occupation I have chosen?

_____

What other goals do I have in mind?

_____

Quick—I want you to grab a pen and highlight everything in this book you feel is important enough to analyze, or where you want to stop and think about the meaning I'm trying to convey. This book was not written just to be read—**I wrote this book for you to interact with it.** Make notes in it; scribble your thoughts down about what you have just read. This is your own book. Make it special and unique.

You have in your hands the **"SECRET"** to finding your own form of success.

You'll find a **CLUE** to this secret hidden within your **daily routine.**

Life is all about choices, and you have made the right choice by deciding to **BUY THIS BOOK!**

To begin with, ask yourself, "How do I want to be remembered 100 years from now?" Then read on, for the secret to achieving that goal.

Contents

FOREWORD

In this book, I will be passing on to you the vast knowledge I have gained about why and how some people have succeeded in life, while others with the same backgrounds have failed. I have carefully studied and analyzed some of the most successful people across a range of different industries, and have discovered the secrets of their success. This is not a matter of skill, talent, or knowledge, but is more about doing things a certain way, so that any goal imaginable can be reached.

"It matters not what someone is born, but they grow to be."

– Joanne Kathleen Rowling
(author of the Harry Potter series)

You first need a clear vision of where you're headed in life, and at least one definite major goal to reach. You need to be able to write down this main goal, and also a variety of smaller goals, whether they are short- or long-term. Having a goal written down gives you something tangible, instead of just a thought you hope to accomplish someday. Goals give you a sense of purpose throughout the day; writing a goal down gives you a better sense of direction, so that you can stay focused on the more important things you must accomplish in life.

Set a deadline for each of the goals you write down. Only by having a list of goals can you clearly distinguish whether you're on the right path or not. If you don't already have a list like this, use the template below to write down the goals you want to accomplish in your lifetime. Start with your short-term goals, then your mid-range goals, before working your way up to those long-term goals. Set a date for when you plan to accomplish each of these goals.

What are my short-term goals? (1 day, 1 week, 1 month: set deadlines for when you expect to accomplish these goals)

_____

_____

_____

_____

What are my mid-range goals? (1-3 months, 1 year)

_____

_____

_____

_____

What are my long-range goals? (1 year, 5 year, 10 year)

_____

_____

_____

_____

Ask yourself, **"What is the most important goal I wish to accomplish, and what am I doing to achieve this goal?"**

_____

_____

_____

_____

Example: My greatest goal in life is to motivate others in the world to succeed.

This book has been written to show you that anyone can become successful, given the correct mindset. No one should place limitations on your thoughts or beliefs. You are your own worst critic, so don't be too hard on yourself. Whatever goal or dream you want to accomplish, know that it can be done—a positive mentality will have a positive outcome. You are the only person who can put limitations on your life. Don't belittle yourself, or your thinking. Think big, make plans, and take action towards your plan every day, so that you can achieve extraordinary results.

"Whatever the mind can believe, and achieve, the mind can conceive."

– Napoleon Hill

Think carefully about the future you plan on having for yourself. Think about what it would take for you to get to that point in life. By visualizing where you see yourself, you can make the right decisions now in the present so that you can get to where you want to be. Make an important decision right now and understand that you will have to retire in your lifetime. Think about what the word "retire" means to you. You are in charge of your own destiny. So take control right now, by not settling for a mediocre lifestyle. Money won't make all your worries go away, but it will solve a lot of your financial burdens. Strive to reach a level of success where you won't need to worry about paying the bills. Always be thinking of how you can improve, in all aspects of your life.

Write down a clear statement, for where you see yourself in 5 years:

_____

_____

_____

_____

Example: I imagine myself as a well-established entrepreneur managing several lucrative businesses.

"The secret to your future is hidden (within) your daily routine."

– Dr. Mike Murdock

Throughout your life, you will be faced with making many decisions. Decisions are just a normal part of life. Be prepared to make the right decisions, because the wrong ones can affect your life negatively.

I would like you to do a simple meditation exercise now. Take a deep breath, relax, and imagine yourself succeeding. Close your eyes and meditate on where you imagine yourself in the next 5 years of your life. Think about all the successful things you plan on accomplishing! Imagine the house you are living in, the career you have, and lifestyle you plan on having! Make sure that when you close your eyes that you're using your imagination! Albert Einstein once said, "Imagination is greater than knowledge!" He made this statement because he understood that there is knowledge everywhere, but imagination is the foundation where all new ideas, inventions, books, and revolutionary things come from. At one point, after all, people thought the earth was flat.

Let no one stop you from trying to make major changes in your life. Be the best you can be in everything that you do, and work harder than the competition. Opportunities exist for anyone who is prepared to work hard, take risks, and sacrifice each day to work on becoming better. Go to sleep later and wake up earlier to work on accomplishing your life goals. We are all given the exact same amount of time on Earth, so it is what you do with that time which will matter the most.

You have made the right choice by buying this book, so that you can access a roadmap of sort to guide you towards attaining your own form of success. Try to be prepared for what life has in store for you. Life is so unpredictable—even if you think you have the best plan, life can always take a sudden turn and head in the opposite direction. That's why you must have multiple plans for your life. Have a plan A, B, and C, and even a backup plan just in case. You are not born into this world with a manual for knowing how to become successful.

"Employ your time in improving yourself by other men's writings, so that you shall come easily by what others have labored hard for."

– Socrates

The most valuable asset that any person possesses is their time. Time cannot be replaced once it is used. Learn how to utilize your time wisely, and do not waste it away mindlessly searching the Internet. Learn a new trade, or a new skill, or something else that is worth your time. Take the "time" to actually try to become a better person, in all areas of your life. Work every day on developing your skills, read more books, and teach yourself new things. Self-education is very important among highly successful people. You need to realize that you are growing smarter every day. Life is all about growth and development. Always strive for a greater form of success, in whatever career or profession you choose, or whatever form of success you're trying to attain.

The future you plan on having is entirely your decision. Don't keep procrastinating when trying to accomplish a goal. Work each day towards the attainment of your main goal. Don't just have your main goal written down on a piece of paper—write down the steps that it will take to accomplish that goal.

Take one hour to think about the dream job you want, and then figure out how to get that job. Try to get paid for doing something that you love doing. Throughout this book, you will notice certain things that I mention again and again. I do this because of the importance of these topics. One of the most important things, and something I cannot stress enough, is setting goals. Setting goals is one of the most important factors for success in life.

Write down a plan for how you plan on achieving success within the next 5 years:

_____

_____

_____

_____

Example: I plan to work each day on finishing my book, so I can educate the minds of millions of readers.

It will be up to you to read and re-read this book as often as possible, until you comprehend your purpose in life and figure out how you can achieve it. Success can only be determined by the individual, so choose your own form of success wisely. I ask that you <u>underline</u> and highlight any part of this book that you feel is important. I have compiled a lot of useful information here that anyone can understand and benefit from, but it will be up to you to act on all your ideas, dreams, and goals in life.

Remember that it is YOUR decision what type of lifestyle you plan on having. Make a mental decision about whether you will choose to be poor, rich, or middle-class. You are the only person capable of changing your mentality and choosing the right destiny. Be sure that you have made the right choice.

Right now, decide what type of lifestyle you plan on having (poor, middle-class, rich, or wealthy):

_____

_____

_____

_____

This is a self-motivational book, and its primary purpose is for you to ask yourself, **"What type of career and lifestyle do I plan on having?"** This is a very important question to ask. You must become focused on your main priorities in life *now*, while you are still young. This book has a lot of valuable information that has not been discussed in school textbooks, but which should have been.

Ask yourself, **"What are my main priorities in life?"**

_____

_____

_____

_____

Example: My main priority at this time is to create a website that will enable my customers to become my salespeople. It will be a multi-level marketing website!

"Be a willing student, for life is one of the greatest teachers."
— Robert Farias

This book explains how anyone can at a young age become an entrepreneur and succeed in life. You must first have an idea, then make a plan, and take action towards that plan, so that you can make that plan succeed! Later on in this book, I will be talking about money, creating wealth, investing, and how to become successful. Don't make excuses in life when striving to achieve something. Whenever you make an excuse, that is the loser in you speaking. Look for opportunities in everyday life situations. There are so many opportunities in life to become successful. You just need to discover your own type of success.

Always be willing to strive for a greater form of success. Don't just settle for one form. Make a list of all the types of success you want to achieve in your lifetime. You can only be as successful as you allow yourself to be. Don't be content with the lifestyles that you have. Be willing to decide how you plan on living for the rest of your life. Be prepared for the future by planning for your life *now*.

This book was written with the intention of helping you move away from where you are currently in life, to get to where you want to be. You are the only one capable of making the most of your life. Benefit yourself by becoming the best you can be. Give 110% to everything that you do. **The most valuable asset you possess is your time.** Make a valuable investment of your time by doing productive things throughout the day. Figure out how productive you are daily, and how much time you waste doing nothing productive.

Concentrate on the more important things in your day first. Make a list of the things you want to accomplish the night before; the first thing you should do when you wake up is accomplish each task one by one. The sooner you realize that you're going to have to provide for yourself in life, and not have to rely on anyone for support, the better life will be for you. Life itself is difficult, but it becomes easier when you have a roadmap that will guide you on this little adventure called "life." Focus on how you can become your own provider. Later on in this book, I will explain in detail what a "provider" is, and what it takes to become one.

Figure out what your good qualities and talents are, and how you can utilize your talents and skills most wisely. We all have hidden talents within ourselves that we never knew existed, and some of these talents can help you to find a career. Find a career you would love to have and do some research on how long it will take you to get that career. Research is the best way to learn about anything. Learn how to become an independent and responsible adult. Make the right choices in your life and you can have a nice, extravagant lifestyle. Your future is completely up to you. You are in control of your own destiny.

"Don't let what you can't do stop you from doing what you can do."
— John Wooden

Never give up when trying to accomplish your goals in life. Try to emulate the person who you admire and want to be someday. Choose a positive role model to look up to. If you have no role model, don't get discouraged—pick up a good book, watch a motivational speaker, or download a motivational podcast. You can find a role model anywhere in life. Believe in what you're doing, so that you can make other people believe in you. Be passionate about the things you want to accomplish in your life. Show your passion by being enthusiastic. And remember to set deadlines for all of your goals.

"A dream that you want to accomplish as a goal is only a fantasy without a deadline."

- Robert Farias

Hopefully, this book will inspire you to become a productive student, who will learn something new every day. Don't get discouraged whenever an obstacle gets in your way. In life, there will always be obstacles that you must overcome. You just need to know that it can be done. Throughout this book, you will see that there are opportunities everywhere in life to become successful. Your life's purpose is what you make of it. You can either be the best, follow the best, or be like the rest. Be authentic. Learn to become a leader. **Be independent!**

CHAPTER 1

LIFESTYLE & CAREER CHOICES!

Choosing the right type of career

Over the years, you might ask yourself the basic standard questions that should be asked almost every day while still in school. One question that you will no doubt be asking yourself is, **"What is my career going to be?"** A career is an occupation you will be stuck with for the rest of your life. If you plan out the type of occupation you're interested in now, while you're still young, you will be able to have a better understanding of what type of career you want while still at school, or before you graduate high school.

Ask yourself, **"What is my career going to be?"**

_____

_____

_____

_____

Example: My career consists of several occupations, but the main job title is C.E.O. (Chief Executive Officer).

Another question you should be asking yourself is, **"What are my special talents and abilities?"** Special talents are good qualities you are naturally good at, or a talent you have acquired over some years of practice. There are many different talents, such as having the ability to draw, write, sing, dance, or play an instrument. Learning how to play several types of instruments at a young age can be very beneficial.

Ask yourself, **"What are my special talents?"**

_____

_____

_____

_____

Example: My special talent is the ability to type 81 words per minute.

Identify what you're good at, and eventually some careers will come to mind. Follow your dreams, and not the dreams of your parents or peers. Don't try to make your parents happy by doing something that they want you to do. The only person you should be thinking about making happy is yourself. Make sure that whatever career profession you choose, it will be something that you enjoy for the rest of your life, or until you can retire from it. You won't know what type of career you're interested in yet, until you research and search for the one that will be the most suitable for your needs. You may also want to do an internship at a job you want to have someday. Applying for an internship can get you the experience you may need to get that job. While working as an intern, you may even get the opportunity to apply for a specific job if you show them your good hard work ethic.

There are so many types of careers available for you in the "job market." It takes little searching to find a well-paying job you consider perfect for the **qualifications you have, which are called skills.** Different jobs usually require different skills; it all depends on the organization you're applying with. There are so many types of skills that one can acquire. Don't be too focused on getting a job—be more interested in finding a career. Later on in this book, I will be explaining the difference between a *job*, and a *career*.

Gaining more skills in life can increase your chances of getting hired faster and getting paid more. The more languages you have learned, the higher you will get paid. Knowing two languages means you're bilingual. Be willing to learn new things, including multiple languages. Learning multiple languages will only enhance your chances of getting hired faster, and it may even result in a pay increase.

Ask yourself, **"What type of skills do I have?"**

_____

_____

_____

_____

Example: I have excellent communication skills, computer skills, and knowledge of managing a business.

Most people have the misconception that a high school diploma will unlock the doors to financial freedom. Nowadays, even a college degree won't guarantee that you will get hired anywhere. There are many people who have obtained their college degrees and are still stuck working in minimum wage jobs. The job market is becoming more saturated every year with college-educated individuals, who are graduating with the same degrees. These are the individuals you will have to compete against within the job market. You must set yourself apart from others in life and gain as many skills as possible, so that your value as a person increases. Later on in this book, I will be discussing what value is, and how there are ways to increase your value as a person.

Understand that a formal education is not a skill. A skill can be defined as an ability, talent, expertise, proficiency, or something that takes a specific type of training. Learn how to acquire many skills in life. The greater and more developed your skills are, the more your value as an individual increases. Whether you want to become a world-renowned psychologist, or some other profession, you must be able to gain as many new skills and specialized knowledge as possible. Don't be naïve and think that you don't need to continue your education, or think that you already know everything there is to know. There is so much more in life to learn. Self-education is one of the best traits an entrepreneur can have. Entrepreneurs are always trying to learn new skills, so that they can increase their general and specialized knowledge and be of great value to society.

If you consider yourself the smartest person in your group of friends, then you must search for new friends. There is a certain saying about this: "You're the average of the five people that you hang out with on a daily basis." Make sure those five people are always pushing you to achieve great things with your life, to become a better person in all areas of life. Try to become friends with people that inspire you to become a more successful person.

Make friends with someone older so that you can gain specialized knowledge from them. Increase your value as a person every day by gaining knowledge.

Ask yourself, **"How much do I value myself?"** and **"What is my self-worth?"**

_____

_____

_____

_____

Example: My value as a person is priceless, since there is no other individual like me. I'm unique; therefore, my value is limitless.

Example: My self-worth is however much I allow it to be. I understand that by increasing my specialized knowledge and skills, I increase my value as a person.

I've learned by observing my peers and colleagues that many people want to get paid a large amount of money for doing the least amount of work. Realistically, that is not the way life works. Working hard to become successful takes a lot of time and sacrifice. Some people may not even understand you initially, as you work on reaching your own form of success.

A lot of naysayers may even try to influence you and put a negative thoughts in your mind. Don't pay attention to what negative people say about your life. If those people are not paying your bills, then you shouldn't have to worry about what they say about you or what you're doing with your life. The only person in life you should concentrate on making happy is yourself. Don't try to please people by doing things you don't want to do in life. Do what makes *you* happy.

Be realistic about setting your expectations for what you want to do in life. Discover the things you're passionate about and follow your heart. If you're passionate about the work you have, then working won't even seem like a job.

Think about famous sports athletes, such as Tiger Woods, who gets paid an extraordinary amount of money to play a sport he loves. So, in reality, it might not even feel like a job to him. He learned a way to increase his value as a golf pro and made money. Similarly, Michael Jordan got paid millions of dollars to play basketball, even though he was kicked out of his high school basketball team for "not being good enough." Some of the greatest athletes have failed, but were determined and didn't give up. Michael Jordan's basketball coach didn't think he was good enough to be on the team. Those people that didn't believe in him are the negative naysayers that come along in your life, telling you that you can't do something. You just have to prove them wrong by showing them that you can do something great with your life.

Don't let these kinds of obstacles get in your way. Know that you can do whatever you put your mind to. Try to find a way for you to do the same as Michael Jordan or Tiger Woods. Follow your passion, follow your dreams, and follow your heart. In life, you will experience a lot of negative comments from people— people who might try to belittle you—but understand that if none of those people are paying your bills, you don't have to listen to them. In life you will always have people who think you can't accomplish your goals, but you will just have to work harder and show them otherwise. Don't make the excuse—there isn't enough time. Wake up earlier or go to sleep later to focus on strengthening your skills. Don't let people who have given up on trying to achieve their own dreams crush you when you're striving to accomplish yours. Set goals, and then set deadlines for all of your goals. I cannot stress the importance of goal setting enough.

Maybe you want to get a career in which you're helping someone. There are so many types of careers that help others, such as becoming a dentist, doctor, police officer, guidance counselor, teacher, coach, mentor, or any other profession based on helping people. Whatever career profession you choose, make sure that you're happy. Being happy is what success is all about.

Even if a person becomes successful enough to become a doctor, think about all the responsibilities they have. Doctors get paid a lot of money because they take years to earn a degree, and also because they have a lot of ongoing responsibilities. You also must realize that a doctor will only get paid for the hours they have available to work in a twenty-four-hour period. Be happy in life and in the choices you make. Find a career you love.

A career choice can also be in starting up your own business. Research what it takes to start up a business. Research is the best way for you to figure out if you can make profit or not in that business. Only a profitable business is worth starting up, so do extensive research before getting involved with anything that involves investing your money or someone else's money.

Most businesses require a lot of time and dedication for them to succeed. One element you need to think about is how there will always be competition in business. That is why you must try and figure out how to create or do something different, new, and exciting. Find your niche and excel at it. Come up with an invention, a book, recipe, patent, or something that will be revolutionary. The possibilities are endless, given the things that a person can do. You can sell a product online without even having to use your own money. There are opportunities everywhere to become successful. Discover what makes you happy and go for it.

Ask yourself, **"What can I create?"**

_____

_____

_____

_____

Example: I can create a book so that I can sell it worldwide.

Try to figure out a way to make money while you sleep. Later in this book, I will explain more about how you can make money while you sleep. I recommended that everyone creates something or tries to start a business.

Be an entrepreneur and start up an online business. You can create a business online, in which you're selling a product. We live in a technological era where selling all over the world is made easy. You only have to create a product and sell it internationally—even if the product you sell is not yours! Sell a product online at a marked-up price and make a profit. There are many opportunities online to generate a revenue stream for your income. Creating YouTube videos where you develop a huge fan base will allow you to sell advertisements on your page, something called affiliate marketing. Don't let anyone stop you from accomplishing your dreams.

Running a business isn't the type of career that everyone wants to have, but starting a business will allow you to create a system in which you earn a residual income.

Don't make the excuse that you don't have the money needed to start up a business. You can use OPM (Other People's Money) if you have a great idea for a business. All ideas start somewhere; so if you must use more than one person's money for your business plan, then get more than one investor to invest with you.

Ask yourself, **"How can I use other people's money to create my own business?"**

_____

_____

_____

_____

Very successful entrepreneurs learn that to produce wealth, you must have multiple income streams. You can have a career while working on your fortune. You can be working on your career full-time during the day, while working on your fortune part-time at night. A job will allow you to have money, so that you can invest in multiple income streams. It all depends on what type of investments you think will have a good return. Talk to someone who has already worked in that kind of business, or if the business is new, then research it first.

In any business you consider getting involved in, you must look at what you think the ROA (Return on Investment) will be. Figure out a way to generate a passive income. A passive income is something that constantly generates money, without you having to do any physical work! This way, you're making your money work for you, rather than you working for your money.

An example of a passive income can be a rental dwelling on which you're collecting rent. Real estate investing can be either a good or bad investment. You must take the time to read and learn about how and what makes an investment good or bad. I can tell you briefly that if something is taking away money from you at the end of the month, then that is generally considered a bad investment. If something is putting money into your pocket at the end of the month, then you have just learned what a good investment is.

11

A house can either be a good or bad investment. If you owe $100,000 on a house in which you live in, and every month you're spending money on utilities, insurance, paying taxes at the end of the year, and during the year you're fixing repairs, then your house is a bad investment. If you think you're paying off the mortgage to build equity, so you can sell it later on for an investment, then you're partially correct. But the house won't be an investment until you sell it and make a profit.

A rental dwelling that is paid off and that pays you rent every month is an investment property. This is generally considered a good asset. You must figure out what is an asset and what is a liability. I briefly touched the subject here, so you can have a better understanding of how the rich spend money on assets instead of on liabilities.

You must diversify and try to create multiple sources of income. Don't settle for just one income stream. Some people may argue that the only way to work is by physically moving something. But work can be defined differently, depending on the person speaking. A rich person will say, "I have my money work for me by having several lucrative investments," while a poor person might say, "There's never enough time or money in a day; I need to find a better job!" It all depends on how you view life. A poor person will always have to trade their time for money. While a rich person uses their money to make more.

Ask yourself, **"In what way can I create a passive income?"**

_____

_____

_____

_____

_____

_____

For a person to earn an income without any capital, that person must exchange their hours of work for money. People work to gain capital, and then use it to their advantage. Try to figure out a way for you to gain your own type of capital, so you can use it to your benefit. You can find different methods of making money work for you, by having several great investments at the same time. Invest in yourself by trying to become self-employed and work with profits, rather than just having a salary and nothing else.

Don't feel obligated to have only one career choice in life. You can work for a company, try to build a company, and have other people work for your company. There are so many types of opportunities in life to do whatever you want to do. You must dedicate all your effort and your time to trying to achieve your goals in life. Think about the time that it would take for you to start up a business. Understand that you will have a lot more responsibility when you own a business. Researching is the best way for you to figure out what type of career you want to have, and what type of business is good to start. Remember to research thoroughly before embarking on your life journey.

Most people try to become *rich* when they should be striving to become *wealthy*. Many people make the mistake of thinking that once they become rich they will keep that money forever. Money management is something that most people learn by themselves. Not knowing how to become financially sufficient using your money could cause "deficit spending". This means that a person is spending more money than they are making. You must know how to budget for yourself, so you won't get into the predicament of being in debt. I will be explaining the importance of money management in more detail, later on in this book.

Having money doesn't mean that your life will be filled with happiness. Money does, however, give you more choices in life. Having more money gives you more opportunities to have more time, more freedom, and more flexibility to pursue the things you love to do. Try to figure out if you're striving to live a successful life filled with opulence and wealth. Or do you not care about how much money you make and are content with living a boring job that doesn't pay you much? If you're reading this book, then I take it that you're the first person I mentioned; someone who is striving to become financially successful by doing what it takes to have more time freedom to do the things you want to do in life.

It's very important to know the difference between being rich and wealthy. The difference between the two is simple. A rich person's money can be exhausted in their lifetime, while a wealthy person can spend all of their money and more in one lifetime. An NFL player can be considered rich, while the person signing those players' checks can be considered wealthy. If you're blessed enough to be born wealthy, try to be charitable to those that are in need.

In life, there will always be people who are more or less fortunate than others. You shouldn't have to worry about anyone else but yourself. Be grateful and count your blessings, instead of looking back at your mistakes. Don't worry or argue about things that have taken place—be more interested in the present and finding ways of making your future look better.

"Yesterday is history, tomorrow is a mystery, and today? Today is a Gift, that's why we call it the Present"

– B. Olatunji

Money won't always make things better, because the best things in life cannot be bought, such as family, friends, love, happiness, and respect. The money will, however, make a significant difference in how you feel, by allowing you to buy the things you have always wanted to. Some of the "poorest" people I have met don't complain about the things they don't have, but are very thankful and appreciative for the things which they do have. I was always told that it's better to give than to receive. Don't let anyone ever tell you that you can't do something. **You must disprove everybody else by showing them that actions speak louder than words.**

What type of lifestyle do you want?

Most people's American dream is to have their "dream job," and to become financially secure by having all their bills paid off. But dreaming about this and getting there are two different things. There are two types of people in this world. The first person dreams the dream and chases it, and the second person dreams the dream and stays asleep. Don't be the second person. Chase your dreams and set goals. If you accomplish that goal, set a bigger goal. Successful people are always challenging themselves to become better, to learn more, earn more, and be greater than the day before. Successful entrepreneurs know what goals they must accomplish the night before, so they start their day early with purpose. Set those goals, so that every day when you wake up, you're waking up to a purpose-driven life. Know the career you want, so you can stay determined in life and strive to have that career.

Be able to see yourself waking up happy every morning. No matter what you do in life, being happy should be the ultimate purpose of whatever you're trying to accomplish. Chasing money will never make you happy since the amount of money you want will always change, meaning that happiness will be a never-ending pursuit. You must figure out what you would do in life if you accomplished all your goals, and you could do anything you wanted. If money wasn't an issue, and all your goals in life were accomplished, what would you be doing in life? This is the question you should ask yourself. Follow your purpose with a plan of action. Wake up every day and attack that plan of action with purpose.

Ask yourself, **"If all my goals were accomplished, and money wasn't an issue, what would I do in life?"**

_____

_____

_____

_____

Choosing the right career can be a very difficult decision to make, especially if you have no idea what type of occupation you're interested in yet. It can be very complicated to decide what type of profession you want to choose, especially when your options are very limited. The higher your education is, the greater your chances of getting hired faster or getting paid more, over a person who has dropped out of school and has no formal education. The only chance you have of getting paid well without having an education or any skills is if your parents or someone you know will give you a job. You can't always rely on someone else to help you get a job; you must increase your skills and qualifications, so you can get yourself a high-paying career.

Some people may think that a $30,000 yearly income is enough money to live on, while others can barely stay within a budget while making over $100,000 a year. **It all depends on what type of lifestyle you plan on having for yourself, and for your children.** I'm not saying that a career that pays $30,000 a year is a small achievement, but if you want yourself and your children to have a nice extravagant lifestyle, then you should strive to get degrees, and acquire specialized knowledge that will get you further in life.

Ask yourself, **"How much money do I plan on making yearly?" and "How am I going to accomplish this goal?"**

_____

_____

_____

_____

Example: I plan on making a million dollars annually with the types of lucrative businesses I open.

Never give up and only settle for one degree, when you know you're capable of attaining at least two or three different degrees. You're the only one who has to live with the lifestyle that you have chosen. Having more than one degree might increase your chances of getting paid more, since you have increased your value as a person, by acquiring more generalized knowledge.

Figure out in your head how much money you see yourself making annually, with the occupation you are interested in. Imagine this with your eyes closed, so you can get a clear picture on the lifestyle that you plan on having. Now, think about how you will achieve your goal of getting there, and how long it will take you to accomplish it. Think about all the steps needed for you to reach that position in your life.

The reason that most people need a job is to make money. The only reason people work is to survive. You must survive by learning how to pay for all your own bills and necessities. Your necessities involve the food you eat every day. If you don't have any bills, then the money you earn is called PROFIT. Most kids don't know the importance of profit, since no school textbook teaches you the fundamentals of earning money and investing—unless you read a great book such as this one, that provides good useful information.

The knowledge that you don't receive in school from your teachers must come from your parents/providers, friends, social gatherings, or through some other information source such as a computer. Most of the information you will learn in life is through observation. Remember that you're the average of the five people you surround yourself with, so surround yourself with positive role models that push you to do better in life. Also, take advantage of the Internet.

The Internet contains an abundance of unlimited information. The answer to any question you may have is at your fingertips. You must take advantage of the Internet by looking at useful information, instead of just mindlessly surfing the web. You must learn how to do productive things online, and get yourself a library card, so you can read anything that you might be curious to learn about.

You must understand that just as the muscles need weights to work out and get stronger, so too does the mind need books to gain more knowledge. Reading is something that everyone should do, instead of wasting time watching your favorite television program. If you watch the same movie repeatedly, then you obviously have no life or have no main goal that you're striving to attain. Watching repetitive television shows is just a waste of time that can never be replaced. Imagine the hours you spend watching television, when instead you could have been doing something productive, such as reading a book. If you were to watch only one hour of television a day, you just wasted 365 hours in a year of your life. That's equivalent to fifteen full days, and the more television you watch, the more days you waste.

Next, I want you to think about all that things that you consider yourself to be weak at. An example can be that you love to procrastinate. Procrastinating is a bad habit that many people deal with, especially with the proliferation of social media platforms. **The mass media has everyone contained in a small bubble, and it's only a few people who are willing to go above, think outside the box, and be greater than before. These are the "doers" of the world.**

I want for you to grab a piece of paper. On this paper, I also want you to write down all your attributes. By writing this down, you can figure out what you must focus your time on, so you can become better at whatever you're trying to improve on. I am going to provide a small template on the next couple of pages, so that this book will be your road map to success. Every time you feel lost, just take out this book and look at all of the things that you have written down.

On this same page, I want you to write down the career choices you have in mind. You can't rely on only one career choice. The more career choices that you think of, the better your chances are of getting one. Make sure you have picked out careers, and not just high-paying jobs. Now I want you to write down one productive thing you will do every day, and sign and date the paper.

Put this piece of paper somewhere you'll see every day; a good example could be on the door in your room. You can also write down a smaller version of your main goal on an index card and carry it around with you all day so that you're able to read it throughout the day. Whatever you do in life, have a plan A, B, and even C. If you don't succeed at first, try again and again. **Remember that you're in control of the lifestyle you want.**

Write down how you will do something productive every single day:

_____

_____

_____

_____

Example: I will do something productive each day that will get me closer to achieving my goal. I will not watch any more TV.

What are my strengths?

_____

_____

_____

_____

Example: My strength includes me solving problems quickly.

What are my weaknesses?

_____

_____

_____

_____

Example: My weakness is the destructive habit of procrastination.

My career choices in life are (Plan A, B, and C):

_____

_____

_____

_____

Example: My Plan A is to sell this book you're reading for the rest of my life all over the world. My job titles will include C.E.O, Business owner,

Student, Salesman, Writer, and Self-Publisher. I'm a self-employed business entrepreneur who works with profits, instead of wages.

Example: My plan B in life is to go to college and get a degree in Psychology so that I'm able to have credibility, and to gain more knowledge by being in an environment of higher learning.

Example: My Plan C in life is to work for a big corporation to earn an income, and then transfer my profit into a portfolio or some other passive investments.

CHAPTER 2

LIFE IS WHAT YOU MAKE OF IT!

It's up to you!

You must realize that everyone has the potential to do something extraordinary with his or her life. But it's going to be up to you to determine what you plan on doing with the life you have chosen. You need to understand that not everyone in life is quite the same, not even identical twins. We are all different due to the simple fact that we think differently. Put yourself in a room full of people. You will notice that everyone has a different unique feature, and a different sense of style. Some people can comprehend things easily, while people who are dyslexic struggle to learn new things. Everyone has different goals in mind. Ask yourself: are you the type of person who knows what goals you plan on accomplishing with your life, or do you just live day to day without a plan for the future?

Just because a person may be extremely intelligent doesn't mean that they will succeed in life. Not all successful people are intelligent, but successful people are determined to accomplish any goal imaginable. A comedian gets paid to make people laugh. If you're funny, then try to become a comedian. Don't let anyone discourage you from making your dreams come true. A person who is persistent about trying to succeed will do so because they have the mentality they will prevail. Try to discover your talents.

Life will become a lot easier when you discover your hidden talents. Life itself is difficult, but you can make it easier by having a plan. You can only get faster, stronger, and better by working on whatever you're trying to improve. You can't expect to get stronger without working hard at it. Everyone has the potential to learn new skills or knowledge, by being dedicated about it. As a child, you realize that not everything can be learned the first time you try. Think about the first time you learned how to tie your shoelace. Just because you can't do something the first time around doesn't mean you should automatically give up. You must learn that trial and error will occur in everything you try for the first time.

If you haven't succeeded at something, it's because you haven't tried enough yet. Don't get discouraged when a brick wall gets in your way. Try to figure out a way to go over, under, around, or through the wall. You can overcome any obstacle that gets in your way. Don't expect to succeed at everything you try for the first time. Every great cook has had to burn a meal to perfect it. Professional athletes, such as skateboarders, have all fallen down, but they still manage to get back up. They say that Thomas Edison failed 10,000 times when trying to figure out how the light bulb worked. He didn't fail 10,000 times, he just figured out 10,000 ways it didn't work.

You must learn to get up if you fall down. If succeeding at everything new we tried to learn was easy, and we could accomplish it the first time we tried, then nothing would seem hard to us. But that's just not the way life works. Life will become easier when you realize that you will have to face a lot of setbacks. Don't let the fear of failure enter your mind. Know that it can and will be done. Practice at whatever you're trying to get better at.

Remember that you're the only one capable of overcoming the obstacles that get in your way. Persistence and perseverance are essential in a successful person's life. Anyone can learn different types of skills, through being committed to whatever you're trying to accomplish. The harder that you work at learning something, the better or closer you become to accomplishing it. You can't always give up when something seems difficult.

Life is full of different obstacles, many of them difficult. Quitting once will only result in quitting twice, and so on. You need to learn how to work hard at trying to accomplish the goal that you're trying to reach. Take small steps towards your goals. Success doesn't happen overnight, and greatness takes time. Rome wasn't built in a day, and in the same way you shouldn't rush your success. Work hard each and every day to accomplish your goals.

Figure out what type of person you are and the person that you want to become. For example, if you're a student and want to become a teacher, ask yourself, "What will it take for me to reach this goal, and how long?" It's very important to know that hanging out with the wrong crowd can influence the choices you make. Surround yourself with smart individuals that will make a positive impact on your life. Look at your life situation you're in. Think about all friends that you hang around with and the conversations they conduct. Ask yourself, "Do my friends know what they want to do with their life?"

Ask yourself, **"What will it take for me to reach my career goal, and how long?"** and **"Do my friends know where their lives are headed in the next 5 years?"**

_____

_____

_____

_____

Example: It will take a lot of dedication, motivation, and sacrifice for me to accomplish all my goals. The majority of my friends are still undecided about what they want to do for the rest of their lives.

Many teenagers are only worried about their immediate situation, whether it is school grades or making the basketball, football, soccer, or wrestling team. You need to realize that extracurricular activities are a big part of the high school experience, but not a very big part of the real world. In the real world it means you will concentrate more on being career-oriented, and focus more on becoming your own provider. The real world is more realistic than the television show on TV. Most people on TV are there because it's their career. They are getting paid to be there. You must question everything that you hear, read, and see.

You can't expect to learn much from watching television or playing video games all day. Use your time more wisely and read more books. Children don't really think about paying bills, since everything is being take care of by their provider. But you need to realize that not everything in life is free. Most things in life cost money. A good example of something that costs money are general living expenses. These are just the typical things that a provider pays for. *You must pay for your house payments, the clothes you wear, and the food you eat everyday. Think about the person currently providing you with these things.*

If currently you're not paying for those things, then thank the person who is. Be more appreciative for all the things that you have. Not all kids are given an allowance for doing chores, such as taking the garbage out, washing dishes, or mowing the lawn. Young kids don't work because there are laws to protect children from working. So anyone who isn't old enough to work must be given money by his or her provider. Not all children have the same opportunities in life. Some children are not privileged enough to be given three hot meals a day, or nice clothes to wear, or have a nice-looking house or car. These may be material things, but understand that everyone has different life circumstances.

You don't get to choose who your parents are in life or whether you are born in an impoverished situation or are poor. None of those circumstances in your life can be changed, and none of those things are your fault. It is your fault in life, however, if you don't rise past poverty. You need to educate yourself to be smarter and make the right decisions in your life, so that you can live a life of comfort and luxury. Try to figure out a way for you to work hard, so you can give your children a better life than what you had. Think about how you will become your own provider.

Below, you will see two questions, for the things you "like" and "dislike" about your life. Try to figure out why you dislike certain things, and how you could transfer some things from the "dislike" section into the "like" section. Everyone will have different answers, because we all come from different walks of life.

Now think about some things in your life you cannot change. A good example is the neighborhood you're growing up in or the parents you have.

What are the things I *dislike* about my life? Why?

_____

_____

_____

_____

Example: I dislike that I am not financially stable yet.

What are the things you like about your life? Why?

_____

_____

_____

_____

Example: I like that there are many opportunities everywhere to become financially stable.

I want you to think about your current life situation and what you're doing to get on the right path in life. Only by changing your situation now can you make the outcome better. Understand that the past cannot be changed, but you are in control of the present, and so you can gain a better understanding of the way your future will look. Be optimistic about your future. Prepare for your future by planning now, in the present. You have the power to choose your own destiny by making the right decisions. You must have a clear image of the occupation that you want.

Everyone will have a different image of his or her "dream career." We all have different personalities, which sets us apart from everyone else.

Remember that 30 people in the same room are not all going to have the same careers. Everyone wants a different type of career. You may want to be a lawyer, singer, drummer, doctor, teacher, engineer, video game designer, chef, artist, designer, personal trainer, author, executive, inventor, owner, or the C.E.O of a company. Everyone in life wants a career in something that they love to do. If you like to paint, then being an artist is obviously a good career to try. If you like to cook, then enrolling in a culinary arts school is something that you should do.

It's going to be up to you to decide what type of career you choose. If everyone wanted the same occupation, then everything would be chaotic. For example, if everyone wanted to become a lawyer, then a judge wouldn't exist. If everyone wanted to become an author and write books, then music wouldn't be created. There would be no doctors performing surgery on patients if everyone decided to be a plumber. That is the great thing about being different and unique. We all want different careers, and that's what makes the world a better place, by having many career choices.

Understand that everyone is skilled and talented in his or her own unique way. One person might be capable of dissembling a car and putting it back together, while another person wouldn't be able to name even four parts of a car. We all have talents that set us apart from everyone else. You must figure out what career will best suit your talents and interest. It doesn't matter if the occupation you're interested in doesn't pay you a lot.

Ask yourself, **"What makes me happy?"**

_____

_____

_____

_____

Example: Teaching people to become successful.

All that matters in life is that you do something that makes you feel good about yourself. Being happy doing something you love is better than getting paid a lot. If you wake up each morning hating the career you have chosen, then change it. What's the point of having a well-paid career you hate waking up to every morning? A high-paying career might motivate you to wake up in the morning, but having more money doesn't mean that your life will be any happier. There are many rich individuals who still have the same problems as a person with no money. Focus on the things you love, and happiness will follow.

Ask yourself, **"At what age do I plan on becoming my own provider?"** Being a provider means you will have to learn how to live independently. When thinking about becoming your own provider, think about the lifestyle you plan on having for yourself. Do you plan on having a nice big mansion with a luxury pool and car, or a middle-class life working every day to pay your bills? Do you plan on graduating from high school and college? Do you plan on having to work for a big portion of your life until you can retire? These are the questions you should ask yourself. The choice is up to you, to decide what type of lifestyle you plan on having. Figure out what type of career you want to have.

Ask yourself, **"At what age do I plan on becoming my own provider?"**

_____

_____

_____

_____

Example. I plan on becoming my own provider when I have enough capital to live the lifestyle I am striving for.

Remember there are many classes not being offered in college. One class that isn't being offered is how to become a successful author. There can be literature or writing classes on how to improve your writing skills, but not a specific class on becoming an author. It's very fun writing your own book, because you can write about the things you know, and have the chance for millions of people to hopefully become inspired by it. Hopefully, everyone who reads this book will feel inspired to do something positive with their lives. Create something, so you're a producer instead of only being a consumer. Everyone in this world is a consumer; by writing a book, you're putting yourself on the other end of the spectrum and allowing yourself to become a producer.

Further along in this book, I will explain to you the importance of trying to become a producer and the advantages that come with it. A salary will only give you a certain amount of money each year. Different occupations pay different amounts, depending on the career that you pick. Having a career will give you a set salary, while having a product will give you the ability to sell it, so you can create a profit. When you create a product, the money you will make in a year all depends on how committed you are to selling that product. You are the one that is going to make the wise decisions of either investing, saving, or spending the money you earn in life. Make the right decision.

The decisions you make in life will be 100% up to you. Nobody will pressure you into doing your thinking for you. You're the one that is going to think for yourself, by learning the difference between making a good choice and making a bad choice. Think about the consequences of a bad decision before you make it.

There are many people in this world who don't think about the choices they make until after the choice has been made. Make the right choice by not giving up when trying to accomplish your goals in life. You must stop making excuses for not accomplishing something. Making excuses is just another way of giving up. Do something productive instead of complaining and making excuses for everything. Successful people don't make excuses but try to find solutions to problems. If you have an idea for solving a problem, then perhaps you can create a patent and sell it. Come up with solutions, and don't focus on the problems.

Everyone in this world has the exact same amount of time on earth, so it's what you do with that time that matters the most. You can do almost anything that you put your mind to. Right now, focus on what needs to be done, and how you will be able to do it. Rather than thinking about what you can't do, focus on the things you *can* do. You must realize that your thinking is the only thing that will determine how your future will turn out. You have total control over your thoughts. So take advantage of this, and think of success! Stop to think about the situation that you're in right now. If you have no money, don't blame it on your background. Being poor is a state of mind; you must think rich in order to become rich.

Ask yourself, "How much money do I have in my bank account, and how can I increase it?"

_____

_____

_____

_____

First identify what you're passionate about in life. Now, figure out how you can transfer that passion into a career. Know that passion gives you the drive to become anyone and do anything that you want to do. You must fill your life with passion and enthusiasm. So take some time to figure out your passions in life. **Passion creates a desire. Desire creates ambition, and ambition creates determination. When determined, you're committed. Commit yourself to becoming the best you can be and more. Commit your life to excellence. Learn everything that you can learn and more! To become successful, you must continually be thinking about how you will succeed in life, and what you will do after that. Remember: success isn't a destination, but a journey.**

CHAPTER 3
STAY FOCUSED!

Use your time wisely!

Time is the most valuable asset that we possess. Time management is very important. You need to learn how to balance your day with the time needed to accomplish certain goals in your life.

Before you go to sleep at night, write down the things you want to accomplish the next day. You can even write down the time that you think it would take you to accomplish these tasks, and set priorities for which tasks you must accomplish first. Start with your highest-priority task, and work your way down on that list. Time management starts from when you wake up, all the way until the end of your day when you go to sleep. Some of the most successful people are very productive people who manage their time wisely and understand the importance of not wasting it.

Write a list of the things that must get accomplished today:

_____

_____

_____

_____

Make sure that you check off the things that you accomplish on that list, so that you are able to see the progress that you've made. Writing it down on paper is a better way to help you remember what needs to be done.

Living a balanced life

In life, you need balance. Don't focus all of your time on working and ignore your own body. Exercising is a good way to maintain an active healthy lifestyle. Learn to be healthy by walking or running at least one mile a day. Swimming is one of the best ways to stay in shape; it's also a very good cardiovascular workout. Working out at least once a month can help benefit your health, and it will also make you feel and look better. Ask yourself, **"Am I as healthy as I should be?"** Restrain yourself from overeating just because you have nothing to do. You need to ask yourself: do you eat to live, or live to eat? Eating should only take place when you feel hunger. You can't expect to get in better shape by only "thinking" about working out. There is a big difference between a person who says something and a person who actually does something. Take action on all of your positive thoughts. You can't expect to finish something without even starting it. **The person who has never succeeded, has never tried.**

Am I as healthy as I should be? If not, what can I do to get into better shape?

_____

_____

_____

_____

Example: I can get up earlier to work out, and eat healthier.

Try to figure what you can do to make yourself physically and mentally stronger. You can become a more intellectual individual by working out your brain by reading more, just as you work out your muscles by lifting weights. **The brain needs to be stimulated continuously by reading more books**. Keep your mind active by playing a skilled game such as chess, or other mental games that challenge your thinking ability, such as a Rubik's cube. Interact with people at social gatherings, such as school, the library, church, or any other place that involves communication between you and other people.

Your net worth can be determined by your net work

In life, you shouldn't be shy around people. Communication skills are some of the most important skills to have. How will you ever be able to meet a best friend, future wife or husband, mentor, or new work colleague if you don't take the time to meet new people? Your net worth can determine your net worth. Very successful people know the importance of having lots of mutual friendships. Having a wide range of friends opens up social connections and helps you get ahead in life. More opportunities arise the more friends you accumulate. Don't be naïve and think that you don't need to have or meet new friends. Be an extrovert and make friends with people in life.

You can sometimes start a friendship with a person you work with. It's always important to know a number of people you can trust. Trust is the key to a good relationship with anyone. It's always good to have one best friend you can communicate with about anything. If you don't have a best friend, then get yourself a dog. After all, a dog is a man's best friend.

Use your time wisely to figure out what type of career would best suit your interests. Be motivated by whatever type of occupation you pick. Strive to be in the number one position all the time, whether it be at playing a sport, or trying to get promoted at work. **Whatever you do in life, don't give up—work hard, and shoot for the moon, because even if you miss, you'll still end up with the stars**.

Use your time wisely by reading about things that can benefit you, rather than mindlessly surfing the web. Remember that achieving your chosen career in life should be your number one priority all the time. You should think about what career you want every day, until the day comes that you actually have one. It's important to realize that one day you will not live at home with your provider. You will have to become your own provider.

A good source of information other than the Internet is books. Great philosophers used to write down their ideas, so that people were able to read their thoughts and learn their lessons. Authors thought that the information they were writing down for the future generations was important enough to be discussed. Try to do your part by reading as much as you can. There is only a slight difference between reading a book and discovering information on the Internet. You can search for anything online in the convenience of your home, while a library book requires you to actually go to a library. You can also download books onto your tablet device and read them from home. Do whichever is more convenient for you.

The last information source other than the Internet and books is adults. Sometimes adults can give you the best type of information, since they have the wisdom that comes from experience. But experience only goes so far. Just because a person is older, it doesn't mean that they are smarter. There are many things that a young person can teach an older person, such as using a specific technological device, like an iPad. You can't remain ignorant by thinking you know everything. There will always be something new to learn.

You must be sure to ask the right person for advice, however. You must be sure that the person who you're getting the information from is actually giving you good information. You can't expect to get good advice from an unsuccessful person, who claims to know the secret of success while not having experienced success for themselves. You must make sure that you're asking the right people for the right advice. Listen to the older, wiser, more experienced person who has made a success out of their life. Next time look at the people giving you advice, and ask yourself, "Is this really good advice?" Sometimes you may want advice on becoming rich, but the only advice that you can obtain is from middle-class people. **Middle-class people will give you middle-class advice.** That is why it's good to read books.

There are many rich millionaire or even billionaire authors who have written down advice, which anyone who reads their book can benefit from. If someone is taking up your time, and you know it's a waste, then figure out a way to stop the conversation from going any further. If someone spends 30 minutes telling your something unimportant or useless, then they just wasted 28 minutes of your time, when you could of ended the conversation. You must cherish your time, since it's very valuable.

But just because a middle-class person makes very little money doesn't mean they don't have good advice to give to you. There is always something that you can learn from someone. My

U.S. history teacher taught me a very valuable lesson in life. He told me to **work hard when you're young, so that you're able to relax when you're old**. I didn't understand his theory at first, but then he explained it in more detail. He told me that if you studied hard, graduate high school, and get a college degree at a young age, you could easily get a career. Most people and even parents give their children the same advice growing up. That advice is to go to school and get good grades, so you can get a good job.

This advice might have been the same advice they were given to them growing up, but it isn't always the best advice. We live in the information era, where we have seen our parents work for big corporations for 40 years of their life. We have also seen retirement pensions plans erased, like when the major corporation Enron filed for bankruptcy. The savings of millions of older Americans money suddenly disappeared.

We are part of a generation that wants to do more than our parents did. We see millionaires coming from all walks of life. You no longer need to have a college education to become a very successful person who accumulates lots of money through the working hard for a big corporation. We live in a time where there is money to be made on all different platforms online. There are millionaires who make money on YouTube through paid sponsorships.

Our generation sees that there are opportunities everywhere to become rich, and that the old method of getting good grades and doing good in school so you can get a good job is part of the past.

Now, I'm not discouraging anyone from pursuing an education. School is the foundation to getting generalized knowledge. But you must understand that generalized knowledge can only take you so far. You must work hard to educate yourself on the possibilities that exist in life, so that you can become more successful.

My professor was teaching us to work hard in school while we were young, so that the career that we'd have wouldn't be hard. A hard career might be something labor-intensive, where you're out in the sun all day. He was simple trying to explain that going to college and getting a good education would be better than just dropping out of high school or college and getting a mediocre job. With most occupations, you will still have to work for a big portion of your life, or until you can retire.

Try to figure out a way for you to work hard when you're young, which isn't your typical normal standard path through life. Be different, be unique, stand out, and make noise. **The more eyeballs you can attract; the more money you can make. Entertainment is a huge industry which lots of people spend money on. People are paying to be "entertained." A lot of**

entertainers think "outside the box." These entertainers are not considered the norm.

My teacher was trying to explain to us the importance of education and how obtaining a degree should make your life a little easier, compared to someone who didn't continue their education. My teacher's main point was for us not to waste all our time doing unproductive things.

You must try to spend as much of your time as possible learning something new. Any time you're not doing something productive, you're wasting time that could have been spent on gaining a new type of skill. **Time can never be replaced.** Ask yourself, "Have I done everything that I've wanted to do with my life so far?" The older you get, the faster time flies, since you get used to doing the same things every day. You get into a repetitive cycle of living your daily routine. Make sure that whatever you do in your daily routine, you're creating success along the way.

Ask yourself, **"Have I accomplished everything that I've wanted to do with my life so far?"**

_____

_____

_____

_____

Example: No, I have not done everything that I have wanted to do with my life so far.

The teacher that gave me this advice was a self-made millionaire, as he had invested in oil stocks years before. He was also at the right age to retire and not have to work if he had wanted to, but he told me something worth knowing and sharing. He said, "Why retire and do nothing productive for the rest of my life, when I can continue to educate the minds of hundreds of children at my own convenience?" He showed me it wasn't only about money, but more about doing something that you love to do and feel passionate about.

My teacher showed me that having money and a degree aren't the only things in life that are important. The most important thing in life is doing something that makes you feel happy, and hopefully something that others can benefit from. My teacher had made a great fortune by having stocks in oil, and was continuing to do what he loved.

Even if you have an occupation which you will retire from in a few years or decades from now, think about how much money your 401k-retirement plan will be worth then. Think about the decrease in the value of money. Money will not have the same value as it did ten years ago. That is why it's important to know how and when to invest. The cost of living is continuing to go up, and the value of the dollar is only decreasing; think about what the value of the dollar will be years from now.

Retiring isn't something that you should be looking forward to. Instead, look forward to finding a career you will love, so that you will dread the day you have to retire. Working should be something that you consider fun, not tiring or boring.

Ask yourself, **"At what age do I want to retire?" Also define what the word "retire" means to you.**

_____

_____

_____

_____

Sometimes you must motivate yourself, so you can motivate others. I never knew that I wanted to become an author, until many other individuals inspired me to share my thoughts and ideas. People motivated me to motivate others. So hopefully, when you read this book, you feel motivated enough to find out your life purpose, and to figure out what type of career you want.

Sometimes all you need is a little motivation to get started in life. Motivate yourself to start doing something new and productive each and every day, so to get you closer to achieving your main goal in life.

Most ordinary people don't know how to become wealthy, since their parents never had the right information to provide them with. It's like older generations passing down middle-class information, or just the wrong information in general. **Usually, middle-class parents give their children middle-class advice**. For you to try and become wealthy, you must figure out how to think beyond any normal standard middle-class person, and do research on how people become wealthy. The key to succeeding in life is to never give up when trying to reach any goal that you have in mind. Everyone has a dream they want to accomplish within their life time. Don't settle for having a dream and not striving every day to accomplish it. Consider your dream a goal and work each day towards accomplishing that goal. Turn your dream into reality. Figuring out on how you plan to accomplish that dream will be up to you.

The occupation of most teachers is to teach students a particular subject in school. How many of these subjects, such as Art, are necessary mandatory classes useful for the "real world?" Always question the knowledge you're given in school, and figure out how it will benefit you in life.

Public school teachers don't get paid an extravagant amount, enough to simply retire at whatever age they feel suitable. Teachers like to repeat information already taught to them. Doctors do procedures that were taught to them by someone else.

Everyone is just repeating something that has been done before by previous generations. The only thing changing is the people. Instead of learning from a teacher, you should teach yourself whatever you feel you should learn. Do something different, and create.

"Formal teaching will earn you a living, but self-teaching will earn you a fortune."

– Jim Rohn

Figure out if you want to work for the rest of your life in a job where you must wake up and work a repetitive job routine from 8am to 5pm. If you don't want to live that lifestyle, then think about what it would take for you to move past that normal cycle of living. It all depends on how long you will have to work.

You don't have to be smart or rich to live a happy life. Do something you love so you can live a happy life. Find the things that make you happy and pursue those. If making money is something that you think will make you happy, then think about a career in which you would be making a lot of it. Having a job will barely earn you enough to make a living, but selling a product will give you the opportunity to make a fortune.

Most people who succeed in life do not succeed because they are smart, but because they had the desire to get to where they are in life. It may take a person years to finally get to where they want to be in life, but the key is to never give up hope and know that you will make it someday. You must overcome any obstacle that gets in your way. You must be persistent when it comes to getting what you want. Be confident about yourself.

Sometimes, you may be a very smart person, such as my father, but not be able to get yourself a different type of occupation because you must support a family, or you don't have enough time to go look for another, more highly-paid career. What ends up happening is that you get content with the lifestyles that you already have, instead of trying to always accomplish much more with your life. Don't settle for mediocrity and stay content with your life situation. Strive to always be accomplishing more with your life. Learn how to gain knowledge in all areas of life. Having a good education is important because school is the key to formal learning, in which you have the opportunity to gain knowledge. Remember to read books to gain knowledge.

Throughout this book, I will be asking you what type of career you are interested in, because that is one of the single most important decisions that you're going to be faced with making. I will also talk a lot about setting goals, since I cannot stress the importance of writing down all of your goals. Be ecstatic about learning new things. Try to learn a new word every day, so that you can sound more intelligent. How you present yourself for the first time to another person is very important. The way you dress, speak, and act makes a big impression on many people. You can't expect to get a career by dressing in shorts, a muscle shirt, and dark glasses. Dress to impress.

Most "average" adults tell their children to do well and strive to be No. 1 in school. School teaches you how to become a good employee, and also other things like being punctual and organized. There are lots of things you can learn in school. But don't just go to school and learn what they teach you there. Go home and learn more. Teach yourself the things that will make you succeed in life. Learn about investments, stocks, real estate, or anything that benefits you in life.

Learn how you can become your own boss. Starting up a business is something that I recommend you learn. You can learn that knowledge from a family member that already had or has a business, or teach yourself. It's always good to get advice from smart people experienced in something that you would be curious learning about. You can use that person's prior knowledge as guidance, to help you to achieve your own form of success in whatever business venture you want to start.

Sometimes a person may have all the intelligence in the world, but lack common sense or the actual knowledge they will actually need to get ahead in life. You must realize that when you graduate from high school and get a college degree, you will still have to work for a big portion of your life, or until you can retire. You must also pay for your necessities during your years in college. These necessitates include the food you eat, the gas you will put in your car, and the cell phone you will need to communicate with people. Hopefully, you're privileged enough to not have to work while attending college, but if you aren't one of the lucky few, then having a job while going to college is something that you will need to pay for all these expenses.

College tuition is also becoming more expensive each year. The only way to pay for college is by getting scholarships, having your provider pay it for you, or by getting a job and working your butt off in both work and in school so you don't accumulate student debt. You might even need to take out a student loan, in which you must pay back after you graduate college. Make sure that the degrees that you're trying to achieve is for something that is in high demand.

The medical field will always be in demand, since people are always getting sick and need medical help. Even if you get a nice highly-paid career, you will still have to work until you're in your 40s or 50s, or even older, until you're old enough to retire.

I'm not saying your 40s or 50s is an old age to retire at. Some people don't ever even get the chance to retire, since they never get themselves an occupation with retirement benefits. If a career comes with a 401k-retirement plan, then that's obviously a well-organized career that will give you good benefits, but only if you work for a company for a few decades. I know I don't plan on doing that, and you shouldn't either! I would rather work a 15-hour shift at my dream job of becoming self-employed, rather than working a corporate job in which you're **trading your time for money.** You should have more goals than to work at a job for the rest of your life, especially if you don't love it. Everyone wants to retire while they're young, but very few people are capable of doing this, so they must resort to working most of their life. You need to see that it's possible to retire at a young age. You just need to have the right plans in place.

Ask yourself, **"How will I be trading my time for work? What plan can I make to retire at a young age?"**

_____

_____

_____

_____

Example: I plan on working for myself and trading my time in return for an increase in sales, and to grow my business more. My plan is to have multiple salesmen sell my book for me, so that I am able to retire at a young age.

The reason why most people work for their entire lives, or until they can access their retirement fund, is because they have not been provided with the right information on how to retire at an early age. They have not been given the tools it takes to become financially independent. For you to become rich or wealthy, you must do some research on how to accumulate your wealth. There is no harm in researching how wealthy people accumulated their wealth. I researched some of the world's most famous wealthy people, and it was to my amazement that I learned that most of their successes did not even require a college degree, and sometimes not even their high school diploma. There are many people who try to find solutions to problems and make millions of dollars. What is your next million- or billion-dollar idea?

Tell me a plan that would enable you to make one million dollars:

_____

_____

_____

_____

Here is one example of a plan: I plan to have 100 salesmen carry ten of my books in a backpack. Their objective is to sell all ten books in one day. My book retails at $14.95. The cost of the book is $1.95, and each salesman will get $2.00 per book sold, which so leaves me with $10.00 profit for each book. If all my 100 salesmen accomplish this task in one day, then they would have sold 1,000 of my books, from which my total profit for the day would be $100,000. If they continued selling them at that rate for the next ten days, then I would have reached my goal of making one million dollars in just ten days.

I will also give you **scenario number two**, in which you don't even need to invest in inventory of a product. Let's say I find a product on a wholesale website. The product on this website sells for $1.00. I then turn around and market that same product on a different website for $11.00. Let's say I sell 100,000 products in one year. Then I have just made 1,000,000 dollars by selling a product in which I don't even own. I can further explain how you can ship that product straight to your customers, and don't even have to buy any stock to make those sales. You only need to have a great idea, a good marketing strategy, a computer, and a good work ethic to successfully become the middleman of sales.

Examples of high school dropouts who have become **Millionaire Dropouts:**

1. Dave Thomas: Best known for his "Wendy's" fast-food restaurants.

2. Johnny Depp: Movie actor, featured in *Charlie and the Chocolate Factory*.

3. Nicholas Cage: Movie actor, featured in *Gone in Sixty Seconds*.

4. Jim Carrey: Movie actor, featured in *Ace Ventura*, *Bruce Almighty*, and much more.

5. John Travolta: Movie actor, featured in *Faceoff*.

6. Chris Rock: Comedian.

7. Christina Aguilera: Singer.

Examples of **Billionaire Dropouts** ("The School of Hard Knocks!"):

1. Michael Dell and Bill Gates dropped out of college to become some of the world richest billionaires!

2. Sir Richard Branson, the owner of Virgin records!

3. Ralph Lauren, Paul Allen, Steve Jobs, Larry Ellison... the list continues.

That doesn't mean that everyone can do the same thing, without getting an education. I don't advocate that you drop out of high school, but I am saying it's possible to become financially successful by obtaining millions of dollars, even without having a high school diploma. Rich people know that to accumulate their wealth, they have to create a high value for themselves as an individual, or have created a product with a high value which they can sell and make high profits from.

Some of the richest people in this world are paid for a talent they have. All sports players are getting paid for doing something that they love. Sometimes a talent can make you excel in your life, but that is not always the case for everyone. So it's nice to have a degree as a nice backup plan.

One thing that school doesn't always teach you is how to become financially stable. **Money is not a subject being taught in public schools.** Only a business class will teach you some information, such as how to budget your spending. A business class will teach you certain fundamentals when dealing with money, but in many instances you won't learn how to become financially stable. Financial education is either taught by your parents; learned from your peers, or self-taught when you get yourself a job, after which you must learn how to budget for your spending. Having a job will give you the ability to create smart or dumb spending habits, since you're in control of your own money.

Some of the world's most famous people—like movie stars, rock stars, or sports stars—have made a fortune from a talent they were given. **You may have the talent, but if you're not putting it to use, then what good is it?** Some of the most intelligent people in life can excel and succeed without a college degree, but not everyone can. Everyone has a different type of goal they want to accomplish someday. Start right now by figuring out your goals. Then take action each and every day towards those goals.

Learning different types of skills and talents as a young kid can help you turn out to become a very skilled person. Hanging around with other skilled people can also help you to become a skilled person. You must take advantage of everything that life can offer. Millions of new things can be learned every day. Figure out how you can become successful. Money is being printed every day, and the goal for you is to try and obtain as much of it as possible.

If you're not happy, strive to get a better kind of occupation than the one you have. There will always be an easier-paying job if you just take your time and search for it, but make sure that it's something that you'll love. You should learn how to make money, before you're even old enough to get a job. It can be very complicated to figure out how to make money without being old enough to work, but there are always side jobs you can do to earn money.

Success

Success can be defined for different people in different ways. How I would define success is doing something that you love. You don't have to get paid a lot for doing the things you love. Happiness is better than being sour and bitter over an occupation that might pay you more. Find out how you can do something that you love and get paid for doing that. Follow your heart and trust your intuition, to get a career you would love to have. Discover what the word "success" means to you.

Success is a state of mind. You need to realize that anyone is capable of becoming successful. Many people make excuses, saying that the only way to become successful is to have money. Other people may argue that they do not have the right resources or enough time to succeed. There are many people in this world who don't even try to succeed, because they are already content with the type of lifestyle they have and are willing to settle for being mediocre. Success can mean a lot of different things to different people. There might be two people with the same careers, and while one may feel as if he or she has succeeded, the other person does not. It all depends on your own definition of what success means to you. Ask yourself, "What does success mean to me?"

What is your definition of success?

_____

_____

_____

_____

Example: My definition of success is to live a happy life!

Success to one person might mean accomplishing a goal, depending on what type of goal it is. Success to other people might mean to become rich and retire young. Everyone has a different perspective on what success means. Have you ever wondered why some people succeed, while others with the same backgrounds fail? By fail, I mean not reaching their full potential to accomplish any goal they set themselves. Try not to make excuses or blame a situation or circumstance in your life for why you aren't succeeding. Remember that you're in control of your own destiny.

Don't think of success as a destination, but more of a journey. You can't become successful by being unproductive throughout the day. Insanity is repeating the same things over and over but expecting different results. You must figure out how to become successful by reading about how wealthy individuals attained their success. You can't expect to arrive at your intended destination without a map or guide. You don't expect to go on a long journey across the country without the assistance of maps or GPS. Life is much the same.

You need to draw up a clear and detailed map of what you plan on doing to become successful. You must make a map of where you are, and figure out where you want to be in the next 5,10,15, 20, and 25 years down the line. On this map, you will write down how you expect to get there. See success in your future. Entitle this map your "SUCCESS MAP." You now know how to make your life become a little more successful. This map is just the beginning of a long journey. Don't get discouraged when you face an obstacle. Just see it as a detour for you to get around. You can't expect to become successful overnight. People that fail usually have no destination, or don't have a map to show them the way.

My "SUCCESS" Map! (Write where you want to be in 5, 10, 15, 20, and 25 years)

_____

_____

_____

_____

Most successful people know where they are headed in life, and how long the trip will take them. Successful people have a clear idea of how long it's going to take them to achieve their goals, because they set deadlines. Setting a deadline for each of your goals is a major advantage for people who expect to accomplish a goal, but forget to set deadlines. Take the time right now to think about one of your major goals in life, and how you expect to accomplish it.

Now think about all the obstacles that you will face along the way to accomplishing it. There will be many obstacles you never expected. Reaching a level of success doesn't happen overnight— it's a long journey, in which you must continually steer your way toward success. You can't expect to see the finish line of a race at the beginning. Have a mental image in your mind where the end of your success map lies, and the obstacles you will have to overcome to achieve success. You're going to figure out what it will take for you to become successful. Make the right choice in life by knowing where you're headed.

You must be an optimistic person, who knows that anything is possible with the right mentality. You're the only one that can put limitations on your own thoughts. Do something every day that will get you a little bit closer to accomplishing your goals. Try to demolish the destructive habit of procrastination. Try using one hour each day to either read something informative or do something that gets you closer to your goal. Remember that you're the only one capable of securing a successful future. Take advice from successful people willing to help you out. Take all the advice you can get but remember to make sure what source you're getting your advice from. *Success can be defined by becoming the person you want to be.* **Now, TAKE ACTION!**

CHAPTER 4

WHAT IS YOUR LIFE'S PURPOSE?

What are you here to do?

Everyone has a distinct reason why they exist. The best thing for you to do is discover what your reason or life purpose is and why you're here on earth. Ask yourself, "**What makes me different from everyone that I know**?" Discovering what makes you unique and talented is the first step to discovering why you were put on this planet. Many successful people succeed because they are striving to accomplish their life's purpose. By having a purpose in life, you're more likely to follow the right path. You're giving your life meaning when you set yourself a purpose. Without having a clear reason why you exist, you will be lost in life, at least until you can figure out what you were meant to do.

Inventors didn't give up when they faced an obstacle that got in their way. Inventors had a thought, and from that thought alone, a desire to accomplish something was set into their mentality. You must be able to envision what you're trying to accomplish by first having a mental image of it in your mind. You need to realize that an inventor is talented enough to have the creative imagination necessary to invent something that did not exist before. Most inventors were misunderstood at first, because what they wanted to create did not yet exist. Others didn't understand, but their idea existed, and it existed first in their own mind.

Ideas are the foundations of all new creations. Just because you can't physically see something, that doesn't mean it doesn't exist. Look all around you. What do you see? Just because you can't see the air, that doesn't mean that air doesn't exist.

What is my life's purpose?

_____

_____

_____

_____

Example: To inspire, educate, and grow in life.

You must believe in yourself—believe that anything and everything is possible. You can accomplish anything that you put your mind to. You must believe this; by believing in yourself you make other people believe, too. You must be confident about everything that you're trying to accomplish in life.

Think about a role model you admire. Now, think about how that person got to be in the position they are in. If the person you admire and look up to is a famous actor, singer, football player, or musician, understand that it took a lot of dedication and sacrifice to get to where they are in life. They didn't just wake up and suddenly become successful.

Successful people have usually worked harder than their competition to become the best they could be. They each had their own specific goal they were trying to reach. They overcame adversity and conquered obstacles to achieve their level of success. They went to sleep later, woke up earlier, and didn't make excuses for not getting things done. You must be willing to go the extra mile, and give 110% of yourself, if you want to become successful.

Most people who look at a famous person don't see where that person started. They don't see all of that person's hardships. They don't see the rejections they had to overcome. People don't see how hard it was get to where they are at in life. Just like most things, success takes time: time to improve and get better, time to acquire more skills, and develop those skills which you already have. Time to face and overcome adversity. Time to become better today than yesterday.

It took a lot of hard work, perseverance, persistence, and patience for successful people to get to where they are. We usually see a person's career high, and not their struggles. Most famous actors, rappers, inventors, video game designers, fashion designers, authors, or celebrities didn't become instantly famous.

They had to work hard by dedicating their time every day to getting better at whatever they were trying to accomplish.

Celebrities knew they had a purpose, a vision of what they wanted to do with their lives. Celebrities have stuck to their purpose and been determined to be the best they could be. However, some famous people are lucky enough to bring their friends into their success, by having "connections." Not everyone is lucky enough to know someone that will give them a helping hand, so the majority of people must work hard from the bottom up. Try to figure out how you can emulate the person you want to become someday.

Ask yourself, **"Am I on the right path with my life in order to succeed?"** Thinking about whether you're on the right path is the first step to making the right decisions. You must concentrate on all the things you need to do to become successful. Even if you're at a level where you already feel successful, think about what more you can do to elevate your level of success. You must get your mind focused on staying on the right path. What you do with your daily routine will determine whether or not you will succeed in life. Remember the quote from Dr. Mike Murdock: "The SECRET of your future is hidden in your daily routine."

Ask yourself, **"Is my <u>daily routine</u> one that I want to have for the rest of my life?"**

_____

_____

_____

_____

"What must I <u>change</u> so my daily routine will bring me closer to become successful?"

_____

_____

_____

_____

"What must I <u>sacrifice</u> for me to reach that level of success?"

_____

_____

_____

_____

"Am I on the right path with my life in order for me to succeed?"

_____

_____

_____

_____

Example: Yes, I am on the path to success!

Most people who succeed in life haven't become successful because they are highly intelligent individuals. The reason why they succeed is that they had the **drive** to get to where they are. These successful people are in full control of what they want to do with their lives. They are in control of their own destiny. They strive to get the most out of their lives. Successful people have a definite purpose for why they exist, and what they want to do with their lives. They follow their life purpose with focus and concentration. Once you figure out what your purpose is in life, you will have a better understanding of where you're headed. **You don't go on a road trip without knowing your destination, because if you do, you will only get lost along the way.** Now that you have a road map to where you're going, hopefully you will get to your destination quicker.

Figure out what you would love to do for hours every day. Maybe you could make your hobby into your career. Try to improve your life physically, mentally, and spiritually. Discover how to use all your talents to discover your life purpose, and learn how to improve all your skills. Life is a game of chess, you must think a few moves ahead, and always be thinking about your end game.

Don't just formally educate yourself by learning at school; use your time wisely by educating yourself. YouTube is a great way for you to teach yourself anything new you're curious about learning. Make sure that whatever you're focusing on, your time and energy is spent learning about something that will benefit you as an individual.

You must try to strive to get the occupation that you want. Do not settle for anything less. Think about a perfect occupation that interests your and will help you to have a luxurious lifestyle. Remember that you're going to work, so pick an occupation you will love having.

Set realistic goals for what you're trying to accomplish with your life and have more than one career choice, so you can have a few options if your first option doesn't work out. You can also make a list of unrealistic goals you hope to someday make into realistic goals. Remember that you can accomplish anything that you want, if you work hard enough to accomplish it.

Have a mental image of what you want to do with your life in the next few years. Anyone can become successful with the right mentality. You just need to figure out a plan for becoming more successful.

Success is a journey. Once you reach your destination, you must continue to stay on the right path. **Every journey must begin with a single footstep.** Take control of your life by getting on the right path. You are the only one capable of misleading yourself. You are in charge of your own destiny, so plan for your future now!

Make a plan

People who don't succeed rarely have a plan to follow. If you currently don't have a plan, then I want you to write one down. This plan will consist of what you're doing right now in the present, and what you will be doing to make your future look better. This will be a detailed plan containing the goals you wish to accomplish within your lifetime. You have your whole life to accomplish your goals. Don't get overwhelmed and think that you must accomplish all of your goals straight away. Start with the short-term goals, then work your way up to the long-term goals.

What is my plan after I complete all of my goals?

_____

_____

_____

_____

Example: I will create more goals to accomplish.

It's okay to have several types of goals you want to accomplish someday, but you must set your priorities straight and focus on one goal at a time. Trying to accomplish several goals at once will only make things more difficult. You don't want to get stressed out by trying to accomplish too many things at once. A useful metaphor here would be, "You're biting off more than you can chew, and you will only end up choking."

Take small steps, so you won't trip. Don't rush things. Learn how to crawl before you try to walk. Setting lots of different goals only gets you sidetracked from focusing on your main goal. You must always focus on your most important goal first.

You need to realize that tomorrow might never come, because nobody can predict the future. So you must do as much as you can throughout the day. Think about the things you want to accomplish before you die. Death is something nobody can predict, so do as much as you can while you are alive. It would be a shame to want to accomplish so many things, but always be procrastinating and never get the chance to actually do them. Do something productive every day, instead of wasting your time.

You are in charge of your own life. You can do as much as possible with the knowledge that you have, and the knowledge you're still learning. Determine the reason why you exist, and what you want to accomplish with your life. Keep thinking about how long it will take you to accomplish your main goal so that you're more focused on finishing it. Never give up! Motivate yourself, so you can motivate others.

What motivates you?

_____

_____

_____

_____

_____

A good way to help you not procrastinate throughout the day is to disconnect the television from its outlet. By disconnecting the TV, you stop yourself from turning it on and wasting hours doing nothing productive. You can also turn off all electronic devices and only concentrate on accomplishing one goal at a time. Electronics can be both a blessing and a curse. They can either help you or distract you—it all depends on how you use them.

Most successful people in this world know the importance of being productive each and every day. They already have their next day planned out by scheduling their days in advance. These successful people are living a purpose-driven life. There are lots of individuals that live day-to-day and do not have a plan for their life, and do not know where they expect to be in a few years' time. Not knowing what you want to do with your life can be very detrimental to a person.

You must make a plan that consists of the things you want to accomplish in your day. Learn to think ahead now, in the present, so you can know what your future might look like. You are the only person capable of knowing what type of future you will have. Don't waste it by not doing anything productive. Time is passing you by every day. You aren't getting any younger! Go out there and explore the world. Take photos and create memories. Travel and make memories with your family and friends. Do something fun. Do something spontaneous that makes you laugh. You can't take life seriously all the time. We will all die one day, so make today count. Don't look back at yesterday. Live life now in the present.

I want you to think about all the thoughts that enter your mind throughout the day. You can even carry around a little notebook, so you can write down the things you're thinking about. This will be a little self-analysis experiment on yourself, so you can figure out the things you think about throughout the day. It can be almost impossible to write down every single thing that enters your mind, because we think of thousands of things throughout the course of a single day.

Analyze your thoughts and your thought processes. Think about whether you're constantly thinking in a positive or negative way. Figure out whether your thoughts about are about your future or not. Within a full day of this experiment, you will discover a lot about yourself as a person. You will have a better understanding of your life situation. After you consciously think about your thoughts, think about the people who you surround yourself with, and their thoughts.

Analyze your thinking... **What do you think about?**

_____

_____

_____

_____

You may be surprised at what thoughts enter your mind. You may be thinking about what to wear, or whether other people are thinking about you. You might be thinking about the opposite sex, or what new movies are out in theaters. You might be thinking thousands and millions of thoughts throughout your life, but how many of these thoughts encourage your growth? Are you a person who thinks negative thoughts throughout the day, or do you think about positive things? Really try to listen to your thoughts, and you will learn more about yourself. If you are a negative thinker, then do something to change that. Listen to motivational audio books or motivational speakers. You can literally re-wire your brain to think positively!

Focus on the important things in your life, instead of the things that won't benefit you. Successful people are always thinking of growth, and what they must do to become more successful. Think about your life's purpose and the plan you have written for your life. Think about this constantly, so that you're re-programming your mind to find ways of getting closer to accomplishing your goal. Throughout the day, think about positive things. By constantly reminding yourself of your life's purpose, you're altering your subconscious mind to figure out a way to get closer to accomplishing your main goal.

You should not be thinking about negative things. Negative thoughts create negative people. You shouldn't be thinking about your problems—you should be more interested in finding solutions. Be optimistic about your life and feel as if you are already succeeding.

When you discover what you want to accomplish, and what type of success you're striving to reach, then ask yourself, **why**. What's your reason for trying to succeed? Is it to gain more money, to be happier, to become more successful financially, or to have more time and freedom? Discovering your **why** is a powerful thing. It will give you a better sense of direction and help you understand why you're doing what you're doing.

You didn't just decide to pick up this book and read this far, if you weren't curious about learning more. You're reading this because you're a very smart individual who wants more out of life. You don't want to live the rat race and be stuck doing the same thing day after day, with no results. **Your future results from your actions today.**

What is your WHY?

_____

_____

_____

_____

Example: My why is to become more financially successful which will allow me to have more free time.

Throughout this book, I have asked you about your goals. I talk a lot about goals because they explain the things to you do in life. Having a goal written down is your roadmap in life. I don't know you individually, but I know that you have a goal to become better than you are now. A goal gives you a purpose for being greater than before, to be smarter than yesterday. So I ask you, what are you doing to get closer to your goals each and every day?

Do you wake up and do something every day that will get you closer to accomplishing that goal, or are you wasting your time by watching television, browsing through social media applications, and playing video games? Do you wake up each morning with a sense of purpose? Do you have a list of tasks that need to be completed each day? You must have the desire to complete any task necessary. Figure out what gives you that desire.

Dreaming and setting goals in life is one thing; you then need to put your thoughts into action by trying to figure out how to make your unrealistic goals become real. There are millions of people who dream about becoming rich or successful. Be different and don't just dream about it—do it! As I have mentioned in the previous paragraphs, all your ideas won't matter if no action is taking place. Remember to take action towards accomplishing your goals. Don't only write down the dreams you hope to accomplish, but also put a deadline to these dreams. A dream or goal that isn't written down is merely a fantasy.

Ask yourself, **"What action am I taking to reach my goals?"**

_____

_____

_____

_____

Example: Every night I'm taking action to finish my book, so I am working towards accomplishing my goal.

Remember to be positive about trying to accomplish your goals. Don't be a negative individual who thinks that everything in life is impossible. You're capable of limiting your own beliefs. Believe that you can make the most out of your life, by having a plan to follow. **With a plan, your life's purpose will become an automatic part of your daily life. You will wake up with purpose, live your life with purpose, and sleep with purpose.** You are the only one who can determine whether you're on the right path. Be happy that you're alive right now and capable of transforming your life into anything that you can imagine.

Remember: *LIFE IS WHAT YOU MAKE OF IT!*

Drive, desire, dedication, and determination!

You must follow your path in life with persistence, passion, and a desire to get your goals accomplished. Think about the four Ds when trying to accomplish anything: *Drive, Desire, Dedication, and Determination.* These are the four words that should be repeated constantly in your head if you are to achieve whatever you're trying to obtain. Remember that there are so many things you can learn. It's always fun to learn new things in life. But you must first have the **DRIVE** to get what you want.

You also must have the **DESIRE** in your mind to get anything and everything that you've ever wanted to have. Build a mental image in your mind of everything that you have ever wanted to accomplish with your life. You must motivate yourself into trying to accomplish your main goals. Remember to set a list of the goals you want to accomplish. Write down these goals and set a deadline for each and every one, so that you can be more motivated to finish them. After you have these goals, the next step is to figure out how you can accomplish them.

Remember that you can have many types of goals, but the main thing is to be focused on your main goal. You must be **DEDICATED** and very persistent in reaching all of your goals. Remember that there will always be different obstacles that get in your way, but you must be willing to take the risk and know that you can accomplish anything you put your mind to.

DETERMINATION is the number one thing to remember when trying to succeed at getting everything you want. You are the only one able to make the most out of your life. Try each day to accomplish at least one goal, or at least get closer to accomplishing one. Remember to live a happy and healthy life. Understand that doing something you love is worth far more than making money but hating life. But if you do something you love and get paid for it, then you have just figured out what your life purpose is.

CHAPTER 5
LIFE!

Be independent

One of the most important things to realize, is that the main person you should count on to be supportive of your goals is yourself. You must be your number one motivator at all times when it comes to accomplishing your life goals. You shouldn't have to rely on anyone else telling you to accomplish things.

Other people may help you in certain situations, but not all of them. You must learn that you're going to be responsible for everything that happens in your life. By figuring out that you're the one who is going to provide for yourself, life becomes easier. Don't put the blame on others for your current life circumstance.

Life itself is difficult. But you can make it easier by figuring out the best way to take care of yourself. When I say the words "take care," I mean financially. **It's very important that you realize that you will have to become financially independent in life. The sooner you realize this, the better you can transition from being a child to being an adult.**

There are adults in this world who still haven't transitioned into the adult stage in life. These are the adults who will continue to live at home, under their parents' roof, obeying their parents' rules, and never try to become an actual adult with adult responsibilities. These are the people who need someone to take care of them. If you are that type of person but are trying to become independent, then do whatever it takes to get there. You don't want to be a thirty-year-old male or female that still lives with their provider. **Strive to become independent as early in life as possible.**

Find a career in which you can earn an income to support yourself. Try to get an income that will allow you to pay all your bills, and still leave you some money at the end of the month. Whatever money you have at the end of the month, you'll be able to either save or invest it. Understand that you're going to have to provide for your necessities and pay your bills. Everything that you want is attainable if you just have the correct mentality of striving for it.

You must be willing to go the extra mile each and every day. The best thing to do is something that you love doing. Many people in life hate the occupations they have. Don't be the person who finds any job available just to pay the bills, and then gets stuck with that job forever. You're the only person capable of figuring out what type of career you'd love to have.

Don't get discouraged and think that the career you might be interested in is not available. Don't make any excuses for not getting yourself an occupation. And don't make the excuse that there is no work available and you can't find a job. You can create your own job by not being lazy and mowing a yard. Grass will always grow; therefore, work will always be available.

Don't make excuses for not finding a job. You must put all of your efforts into getting the career you want. Don't waste your time all day doing nothing productive. There are many people in this world who live without goals. **These people wander throughout life lost. You must have goals, to know what you're striving for.**

You must put all of your efforts into doing something every day that will bring you closer to your goals. Try to emulate the person you admire and wish to become someday. If you cannot figure out something productive to do, then read a book. There will always be something interesting that you can do.

Think about how interesting and productive your day would be if someone were to follow you around with a camera and document a full day of your life. Now, imagine if this went on for a week, a month. Would you be pleased with the results of the footage, or surprised that you are wasting a lot of time doing nothing? What would you change if you could change anything about your daily routine? What would you add and what would you take away? These are questions that you need to ask yourself.

Most people that succeed in life are productive, literate individuals who continuously want to accomplish more, do more, learn more, and be better than yesterday. Don't settle for a mediocre lifestyle. **And most of all, learn to be independent; being independent is what the real world is all about**. Being independent means that you have a job, in which you pay for all the things you want in life.

Is a house an asset or liability? Good debt vs. bad debt

Debt can be both a good or bad thing, depending on the person speaking. An example of good debt can be an asset you purchased. An asset makes you money. One example of an asset is a house. A house can be considered either an asset or a liability. It is an asset if it's putting money in your pocket, such as a house than is giving you a rental income. A house not generating you any income, which only generates expenses, such as property taxes and insurance and mortgage payment is usually considered a liability. This is the case for most home owners. Home owner's have to constantly be paying the bills, property taxes, and insurance, and whenever something breaks needs to be fixed.

Another example of an asset can be an apartment complex. If an asset is generating more income than expenses, it is usually considered a good asset. If you get yourself a mortgage on an investment property, then you just created a good debt. If you get yourself into a loan which you cannot pay off, then you just created a bad debt for yourself.

Buying a home is one of the greatest investments you can make in your life. But remember that it can be an asset or a liability. It all depends on the person. Remember that anything that takes away money from you at the end of the month is usually considered a liability, while something that puts money in your pocket is usually considered an investment. Figure out what puts money in your pocket, and what takes it away.

The wealthy know what assets are and buy them and use them to their benefit, while the poor only buy liabilities.

What is an investment?

_____

_____

_____

_____

What is a liability?

_____

_____

_____

_____

To complicate things but educate you a little bit further, I will explain to you how a house can be both a liability and an investment. Most people have the misconception that a house will always be an investment. Think about the housing market crash of 2008. Multi-million-dollar homes had gone down in price, and lots of people lost their homes to the bank.

Imagine making a purchase on a home valued at one million dollars in the year 2000. You're paying the mortgage on a house that was appraised at that price. Then the housing market takes a hit, and now that same house is valued at half of the loan price of the mortgage. What usually happens is that people no longer find value in that house, and so they stop paying the mortgage and lose their house. You can also think about how when the value of the house went down, then so too did the initial investment. That is, if you think that all houses are an asset.

Let me give you another scenario. Let's say you're paying off a mortgage of a $100,000 house over 30 years. Within those first ten years, you have paid $64,000 towards the mortgage. But out of the $64,000 you paid, only $10,000 went towards paying off the principle of the payment, and the other $54,000 went on interest. You just spent ten years paying $10,000 dollars off a mortgage.

Compound interest is something that we're not taught at school, but credit card companies and banks know exactly how it works. Whenever you're in the market to purchase a house, first look up a mortgage calculator that will explain how the interest rates work. Most people don't understand interest and how it works, unless they learn about it on their own, or someone explains how it works.

Now that I have explained to you how a house can be a liability, let me explain a few scenarios where a home or business can be considered an asset. Real estate is something that most rich entrepreneurs acquire in their lifetime. But these entrepreneurs don't acquire real estate and leave it sitting there as a liability. They know how to make their money work for them, and they do the same thing with real estate.

Let's say that you own a home. The only thing you must pay for is if something needs to be fixed in that house, such as a small or large repair, and the taxes at the end of the year. Let's say that you rent out that house. Whatever rent you're collecting has automatically turned a house into a rental property generating a passive income. There are also tax breaks available to landlords who own homes, so they can write off certain expanses when it's time to do their taxes.

Another type of asset apart from a home is a residential business or a commercial building. By running a business from your residential home, you can make money in whatever business you own. You are not only able to produce an income out of your real estate asset, but also there are again tax advantages for doing business out of a residential or commercial building. Remember that whatever is bringing money into your pocket is usually considered an asset. For you to become more financially successful, you must figure out how to accumulate more assets in life.

Don't make the excuse that you don't have enough money to accumulate assets. Work hard, earn money, make an investment and start getting yourself some assets. Don't let any negative thoughts about you becoming successful enter your mind. If you don't have a good work ethic, then you will end up working for someone who does. You will be working for someone else's dream. So work hard, take action, and be determined to acquire assets in life.

Don't settle for mediocre

Having a job may pay you a salary, but then you won't have much time left for trying to focus on your career. Try to get a career first. People may think that being a teacher who get's paid $30,000-$40,0000 a year represents a good career. Think about it for a while: do you think a teacher getting paid that amount can ever afford life's luxuries, such as a multi-million-dollar house, or a nice expensive car? Those may be material things, but there's no harm in that if you work hard to earn them.

Being a teacher is a career for someone who wants to settle for a mediocre lifestyle. These public-school teachers also teach the majority of schoolchildren. How are you able to figure out how to become financially successful if you are being taught by an educator who doesn't even earn a six-digit yearly income?

Job, career, or occupation?

Many people have the misconception that a job and career are the same thing. You need to realize that a job is temporary, while a career is forever. A job is something that most non-skilled people acquire during high school, or right after that. Nothing is wrong with having a job, but don't turn that mediocre job into a career. A job usually involves little to no skills, while a career may involve specific training or a higher level of education.

Most careers take years of going to school to get into. A good example of a job is working at a fast-food place, whereas a career would be something like being a lawyer. I once heard that "job" is an acronym for "JUST OVER BROKE." I don't think this is entirely true, but it seems to make sense. It's not like you're broke, but it's barely enough to get by and pay your bills. You must find a career in which you can make profit after paying all your bills.

Strive to have an extravagant lifestyle. Don't settle for anything less than the best. You're the only one capable of figuring out what type of lifestyle you want. Now you know the difference between having a career and job, so I will discuss what an occupation is.

An occupation is a way of providing the necessities required for you to live. This means that a career and job are both two different occupations. You can either have a low- or high-paying occupation. You must make a clear distinction in your mind that a career requires training, experience, and years of school, while a job doesn't require any technical training. Figure out for yourself how you can get a highly-paid occupation so that you can have a nice, luxurious lifestyle filled with opulence. Don't get yourself a low-paying job, and be stuck with it until you die.

Set your standards high when searching for a career. Jobs usually train you for whatever specific task you have to perform in that occupation. Job training may take a few hours—for example, learning how to work a cash register—or it may take a few days. It all depends on how difficult that job is. Sometimes jobs don't require that much mental ability but require more physical labor.

You must figure out for yourself whether you plan on having a job or career. Only you can make the right decision. I would recommend that you search only for careers and leave the jobs to inexperienced individuals. You can sometimes have more than one job if your schedule allows it. This means you will be giving up more of your free time, but you will also get paid more.

You can also have both a job and a career. If you're a hard-working person that loves to work, then you can have two careers, instead of having two jobs. A good example of having two types of careers would be a person who has two different degrees. For example, a person with a teaching degree and also a doctoral degree can have two careers. They can be a teacher Monday through Friday from 8am-5pm, and work at the hospital at nights and weekends. This would mean that all that person's time would be spent working, but it all depends on what level of work you want to take on as an adult. The level of commitment varies from person to person.

There will always be people in this world who have nice high-paying jobs, but never seem to find themselves a career, because they become content with the lifestyle that they have adjusted to. Learn to become successful by doing something that you love. Even if that occupation doesn't pay you much, if you get a lot of satisfaction from it, then make it into your life long career. Figure out whether you're looking for a job or career. The choice is up to you.

Write a book!

You can also use some of your spare time to write a book. A book is a good way for you to write about something that you know, or something that you feel is interesting, and is worth sharing! Hopefully, you will write about something that will inspire millions of people. By using your spare time to write a book, you're allowing yourself to generate a passive income.

Passive income means that you have figured out a way for your money to work for you. Other books can give you more information on that, but here I am trying to show you that anything is possible. The main reason why I would recommend that you write your own book is to make another way for your money to work for you.

Writing a book is almost the same as running a business. You must first have an idea. Then you must turn that idea into an actual book. So, you must create the product, which might take days, months, or even years to write. Once you have finished writing, then you have to pay to have it organized professionally. Remember that you can always pay other trained, skilled people to handle any specific task you can't accomplish on your own, but you need enough money to pay for that. There will always be people who are the experts at solving a certain problem. These are the people you can pay, which will save you time, so that you can be working on improving the things that you are good at. Find people who will be of good use to you. And finally, you would be ready to produce the book so that it is available to sell. And whatever you write about, make sure that you're passionate about it.

Next is the marketing stages after you have written your book. There are many great opportunities when you write a book. I would recommend to self-publish, since you would keep the majority of royalties. There are many great advantages for publishing a book. One of those advantages is that you have the opportunity to sell the book while you sleep. All you have to do is upload the PDF on Amazon's website, and they will be able to sell it for you. This term is called Print-On-Demand. Print on demand means that you don't have to acquire any inventory. Amazon will print it, bind it, and ship it for a small fee. You can literally be at home marketing your book on your laptop, while a big publishing company or big website does all the effort to create the actual product for you to sell and make money. You just have to sit back, and wait to collect the check, or get it directly deposited into your account.

The information I have shared so far in this book was important enough for me to take the time to write down, so that someone else could benefit from the things I wish I had read about while still in high school. I hope that I inspire at least one person to become a successful person.

The provider (parent/whoever raised you)

The provider is usually the person who has raised you ever since you were a child. Children are not capable of providing for themselves, so they typically live with their parents. Usually, your providers are your parents, but not everyone is privileged enough to have both parents, so I like to simply call this person "THE PROVIDER."

The head of the household doesn't have to be male. Anyone can become the head of the household and be the provider. It's better when both people in a relationship work to become independent, so they won't have to rely on each other for financial support. Try to figure out a way for you to become your own provider, so you won't have to rely on anyone else for financial support.

In life you must work hard to become successful. Successful people understand that the harder that they work, the more successful they become. The harder you work, the better your chances of getting promoted faster. If you strive to achieve something, only you are able to accomplish that desire. Remember that anyone can turn their dreams into goals, just by being determined.

The first thing you have to instill in your mind is that you must work hard and never give up. Think to yourself that everything and anything is possible. Don't let failure enter your mind. Everything you see around you started off as an idea. You can't always rely on your provider to be your only source of income. It's important when you get old enough that you get yourself a job, so that you can be responsible about learning how to manage your money.

When you first start living on your own, you quickly realize the responsibilities and duties that you must fulfil. Men usually want to become independent in order to support a family, while women usually learn how to do motherly things such as cooking and cleaning. This is just a stereotype, which people must readjust in their minds. Men and women both must take responsibility, by learning how to cook and clean for themselves, and be responsible for paying the bills.

The provider usually has to take care of all payments, such as the bills for the house and the car payments; this requires a lot of responsibility. The older you get, the more you learn that you need to make sure that your responsibilities are being taken care of. I want you to think about who is currently paying for these things in your life, and I want for you to thank them!

What must I do in life, so I can become my own provider?

_____

_____

_____

_____

CHAPTER 6

MONEY MANAGEMENT!

How well do you handle money?

Money management is one of the most important contributing factors that can make you either a financial success or a failure. In life, we must be in control of our finances and figure out how to control our spending habits. We can choose to either make good or bad spending habits. Determining whether you are creating good or bad habits will depend on you as a person. How you manage money plays a very important role in how your future will unfold.

You must distinguish whether you are someone who can make smart budgeting decisions, or if you like to spend money without thinking about the financial consequences. Do you know exactly how much your bills come out to, and when each bill is due? Or do you spend all the money in your bank account and overdraft your account every single time? Do you know how much money you need in order to pay your bills, or do you not care and swipe your bank card for every good deal you see at the store? You need to realize that in order to buy the extravagant, high-priced items you want, you must make enough money for those items so you won't put yourself in debt. Getting yourself into debt is a lot easier than getting yourself out of debt. Money management is an essential part of life.

To be able to manage your money, you must understand what budgeting entails. There are computer software programs with spreadsheets that allow you to budget your finances easily, by providing different categories where you can input the information and it then self-populates the rest automatically. To give you an example of a simple budget plan, I want you to write down your income. Write down a list of all your bills. If you have no income or bills, then you can write down the future income you want to have from your career, and also write down a list of all your future bills. By writing down your bills, you will start to better understand what it takes to manage your money, and how you plan on spending it wisely. If you can't get into a good habit of money management at a young age, then you will probably get yourself into some serious debt later on in life.

It's very important to know how to distinguish between **needing** and **wanting** something. Knowing the difference between the two will be very beneficial in learning how to manage your money. Most materialistic items can be considered wants. An example of a want might be a new technological device, such as the newest TV or newest cell phone that has just come out. The main things you really need are food, clothes, and shelter. Anyone can make a lot of money, but only a few people who make a lot of money know how to manage it well. Which type of person are you?

It's important to know how to be financial literate from a young age, so that you are more knowledgeable when it comes the time when you have to save, invest, or spend money. Think about all the income you're earning. There are several different ways you can earn your money. Working a corporate job would seem the most rational way, since you get paid an hourly rate. If you're young enough that you cannot yet work, then your provider pays for most of your necessities and more. Don't rely on anyone to support you in life. **Work each day on becoming financially independent and work each day on becoming your own provider.**

Then there are unconventional ways to earn money, in which you must be an entrepreneur. Go against the norms of society and be different—do something creative that will make you stand out from the crowd. Invent something, create something, such as a new business. An entrepreneur takes risks by starting up a business. Don't let naysayers tell you that it's impossible. There are people who were called crazy before they were called a genius. They were crazy when nobody yet understood their vision. Successful entrepreneurs have vision. Make sure you understand that in order to become financially

successful in any business, you nee to learn on how to balance your spending habits.

Learning how to budget your money is a very important stepping stone in life. Learning how to become financially responsible at a young age can be a challenge to some people. It all depends on how disciplined you become when saying, "no," to temptation of buying something you want. Just because you can afford something now, doesn't mean that you can afford that same item later. An example of something you can afford short term can be considered a car. You might think that just because you have the down payment, that you'll be able to afford the car payment.

Make sure that you see the long-term investment in anything that involves you spending your money. If you can't afford a car payment, then you are going to end up getting the car repossessed. If you have a credit card that you can't afford the amount you are charging on it, then you'll have bad credit. You have to look at the pro's and con's of everything you do in life. Short term decisions can have long-term affects.

Good money management skills teach you responsibility as a young adult, so that you can make better decisions when you grow up. It's very important to learn how to budget your money, so you can distinguish the things you **should** buy from the things you **want** to buy. It's important to learn what to spend your money on, so you don't get yourself in the predicament of always being in debt!

Make a list of the things you need in life:

_____

_____

_____

_____

Now, make a list of the things you want in life:

_____

_____

_____

_____

There will always be additional jobs you can do to earn money, such as cutting yards, cleaning houses, painting houses, moving furniture, or selling lemonade. Most side jobs require nothing other than hard work and dedication. Most people don't think that cutting yards will make them very much money, but that is only because these people haven't tried it. Sometimes people are just too lazy to work for their money.

Learning how to budget your time and money are crucial life skills you need to focus on. Working at a minimum wage job will usually take up a lot of your time and energy, while you only get paid a small fraction of the money the company you work for will make from you. The bigger the company you work for, the higher your salary should be.

The lifestyle you want will be determined by the choices you make in life. You must decide for yourself how much money you plan on being paid. Switching from job to job will not raise your pay significantly, but having several degrees will give you a higher probability that your annual salary will increase. Don't procrastinate and wait until tomorrow to figure out what you want to do with your life. Take action in your life and start doing it now!

I want you to think about in your head how much money you want to make annually; in whatever occupation you have thought about having. Now ask yourself, **"Is this the amount of money that I want to be making for the rest of my life?"** The sooner you know on how much money you want to make, the easier it will be for you to make the right changes in your life for you to be able to reach those annual earnings.

Now, I want you to think about how much money you see yourself making in the next five years. Do you see a significant increase in the next five years, or only a slight increase because of a promotion or raise? These are hypothetical questions, so that you can have a better understanding about whether you're making the right choices now in your life. Remember to think far into the future, so that you are better prepared for the present.

Ask yourself, **"How much will I be getting paid five years from now?"**

_____

_____

_____

_____

Example: I will be getting paid more in five years from now, since I will be in sales, and my annual income will be determined by how hard I want to work!

I now want you to visualize how your future will look ten years from now. Close your eyes so that you can have a clear image. Thinking five years ahead can be difficult, so thinking ten years ahead is an even greater challenge. But the reason I am asking you to do this is to challenge your mind, and to be prepared now in the present to make the right decision about where you're headed.

I ask you to think ten years ahead so that you can make sure that you're heading in the right direction. Picture the houses that you want, the car you will be driving, and the occupation that you have chosen. Think about all obstacles you faced along the way, and also think about who you plan on sharing your time with.

Think about whether you're married already in your life, who you want your partner to be, and whether you have any children. Do you like the lifestyles that you have imagined? Are you financially stable, and paying all your bills on time? Do you have any extra money saved up in the bank, so that you can take a vacation whenever you want? Don't only dream about this, but work on achieving this goal. Prepare yourself now by making the right decisions.

Think ten years from today, and think about all things that will change in your life:

_____

_____

_____

_____

Example: I imagine a life filled with opulence, love, and happiness.

Are you financially literate?

You must have a clear vision of your main goal in life, so that you won't get easily distracted and sidetracked by the smaller things in life. You will go to sleep trying to accomplish that goal, and wake up with a purpose. Always be setting different goals, so that you live life with purpose. Ask yourself, **"How am I building my wealth every day?"** By answering that question, it gives you an advantage and a head start over those people who don't realize that they must focus on building their wealth every day. You must think about how you're building your wealth daily if you want to increase it. Many people are content with the lifestyle they have, while others are more curious to discover a way to make their annual income increase. It all depends on what type of person you are.

Ask yourself, **"How am I building my financial wealth every day?"**

_____

_____

_____

_____

Example: I am building my financial wealth everyday by completing this book, and by having the chance to sell it to millions of people, so that they exchange their money for my product!

Most ordinary people don't understand the importance of being financially literate. Being "financially literate" doesn't mean that you know how to read money. It is just another way of saying you know how to budget and invest your money. Budget your spending by being financially literate can be a very complicated process in life if you are not taught this basic skill. It's very crucial to be knowledgeable about the subject of making and spending money.

Anyone can make money, but you also need to learn how to manage it. Learning how to manage your money and making sure that you pay your bills at the proper time, is crucial. It's very important to learn how to budget properly, especially when living on your own. Don't make the mistake of thinking that your provider will always be able to take care of everything. You must learn how to be independent. Remember that responsibility for the bills being paid on time will one day be in your hands, when you leave your provider's house.

Think about the situation that you're currently in. Think about all bills that you want to have as you progress in life, and how you are going to be able to afford them. As a child, you don't realize the responsibilities that a provider has. Providers make sure that you have light in your room to see at night, that the hot water is running to take your daily showers, and that the house payments are being taken care of so that you can have shelter.

The older that you get, the more you become aware that everything important costs money. Money is the machine for making the world go around. Like I've said before, money won't make a person happy. Money is just the tool that will allow you to have more in life. You can be poor and complain about your problems, or be rich and find some solutions.

Ask yourself, **"Am I financially responsible?"** Financial responsibility means you can live on your own and pay for all your bills without getting yourself in debt. Don't get a credit card if you will not be able to pay it off.

Keep your spending within the limits of the money you are making and try to not get into the habit of putting things on credit. You either have the money or not. You don't want to have to owe money on your credit cards, simply because you were not able to manage your spending habits, and didn't understand the concept of high interest rates.

If you don't understand what the APR in interest rates means, then educate yourself on those things. You can use a credit card with a high interest rate, where you end up paying double what you originally thought you would spend. Remember: buy the things you **need**, not **want**. Decide which things you can afford.

Let's say that, hypothetically speaking, you owed $3,000 dollars in credit card debt. You don't want to buy a $1,500 dollar flat-screen high-definition television when you already owe $3,000 dollars in credit card debt, or any other debt for that matter. Don't get yourself in debt by buying things you already own, such as a TV. That television would be half the debt that you already owe on that credit card.

Learn to make wise decisions when it comes to credit. Your credit is how many companies assess your ability to manage your money. Credit is a very important tool that can affect you across all aspects of your life. Having bad credit can affect your chances of getting a job, buying a car, a house, new furniture and appliances, and it can determine whether you pay high interest rates or not.

Usually people with good credit scores get better "deals" for buying all those things I just mentioned. Taking care of your credit is important. In the next chapter, I will explain in more detail what a credit score is, and how it can affect you. I will also explain how you can improve your overall credit score.

The decisions that you make in life will affect you one way or another. It's okay to treat yourself to something nice at times, but only if you can afford it. You don't want to buy yourself a $600-dollar TV and a $400-dollar watch if you have only $1,000 dollars in your bank account.

Make smart decisions when it comes to how you spend your money. Remember that the rich spend money on investments and on assets. Don't make the mistake of buying a useless commodity.

Buying those items will leave you with no money, just a new watch and TV. Be smart about the decisions you make.

Getting into debt is like digging yourself a hole, and then being trapped inside that hole. The more debt you accumulate, the deeper you're digging your own hole. It also isn't smart to add on other payments when you are already in debt. Being in debt is one thing, but adding another payment to your monthly expenses is simply ridiculous.

A good metaphor would be to imagine that you're digging a hole, and that hole is already so deep that it's up to your own height. When you add an extra payment to your monthly expenses, it's like you created a rain cloud, and it's about to start to rain in on that hole. You must figure out a way to get yourself out of debt sooner rather than later.

The longer you procrastinate, the bigger the problem gets. Take care of a small debt problem before it escalades into a worse situation. Pay off the credit cards with the highest interest rates first. You can also pay off your smallest debt and work your way up to the biggest debt you have.

Talking about credit is something that high schools never taught me, and so I took the time to study it myself. I recommend that you also study credit and how it works, since credit is your financial report card as an adult. The higher your credit score, the more banks will see you as a potential client and as a responsible person.

Retire young, retire rich! Increase your value

You need to first retire in your mind, before you can retire in reality. You are the only one capable of making yourself retire. Make the best decision for yourself and understand that you need to be your own provider. A fixed salary is a good way to make a living, but how long will it take you with a career like that to finally retire? Are you going to work at that company until you're in your 50s or 60s, or even 70 years old?

Do you plan on being in excellent physical condition, where you are able to actually enjoy your retirement? I want you to think about retiring early in life, and work on securing passive income streams throughout your lifetime.

A passive income can allow your money to work for you. An example of a passive income could be renting out a house and collecting the rent. Whatever passive income comes to your mind, figure out a way to capitalize on it. A passive income is always a good investment to have. If you don't understand what passive income is, then pick up a good book about investments that will tell you all about it. Read a good business book that will give you ideas on which types of businesses will be profitable, and which types of investments to make.

The work-1,000-hours-in-one-day principle

Have you ever thought about what it takes to work one thousand hours in one day? Most people may think that it's impossible to work one thousand hours in one full day. But these are the people who don't understand what it takes to become rich. **Very rich and successful people know the secret of multiplying their hours. Rich entrepreneurs use other people's time.**

OPM, or "Other People's Time" is a principle that most ordinary people don't understand. You need to understand that this is one of the little secrets that make a rich person so successful. Have you ever thought about big corporations, and who works in them? Think about a very large and successful organization. Does the person who owns that organization work there every day? You'd be surprised to learn that the boss probably works the least number of hours at his own business. Major corporations are very successful for three reasons.

Before I explain these three things, I want you to guess how you can work one thousand hours in one full day:

_____

_____

_____

_____

Here are the three reasons that big businesses succeed even without the boss being there and working hard at that business.

Rule #1: Big businesses succeed because of systems. Systems play a very important role in most successful businesses. Without a good system, a business will fail. Good systems are the reason big monopoly companies globalize and expand their business. They create a system that manages itself, and multiplies. As long as there are the right people in place to manage that system, you can multiple it and create a very profitable business venture in any state.

Rule #2: Successful businesses provide good value or have a product or service which they can sell. Most thriving entrepreneurs, in whatever industry they are in, have a great product or service which their employees can sell.

Rule #3: A great business requires a lot of employees to run it. Great business owners buy their employees' time. They can multiply their work hours each day by hundreds of thousands of hours. The businesses are using the resources of other people's time, so they can make their businesses excel and succeed even more.

This last rule shows you that if you don't wake up every day and work hard to chase your own dreams, the chances are that you'll end up working for someone else's. I asked you to guess how to make more money within the 24 hours that are available to you each day. Lots of successful people understand that they can fit one thousand hours into one day. The answer is a well-kept secret that few people talk about.

This secret is also something that very successful business entrepreneurs try to implement with their own businesses: they try to create an excellent sales team. I will explain to you in detail how you can work one thousand hours in one 24-hour day. This concept might seem crazy to you if you have never heard of the possibility of getting one thousand hours of work done in one day. It's simple to do this when you have one hundred workers, and you "borrow" or pay them for their time. You use ten of their hours a day, to do a job you need to get done. So by having one hundred workers, you use their time to your advantage. I have now explained to you the one thousand hours in one-day principle.

Whatever idea you have, whatever occupation you want, my advice to you is this: just do it. Live life each day as if today was your last day here on Earth. If you knew that you would not be alive tomorrow, would you waste all that time doing nothing? You aren't guaranteed a next day, so take advantage of your time now.

Don't procrastinate and say, "I'll do it tomorrow." Remember that yesterday's tomorrow is today, and that tomorrow might never come. Try to figure out how to retire young, or have a career that you would love to have for the rest of your life. I will retire at a young age because of the entrepreneurial spirit I have, but sharing my knowledge with you is even better. Ask yourself, **"How valuable am I as an individual, and how am I able to increase my value daily?"**

How can I increase my value daily?

_____

_____

_____

_____

Example: I can increase my value daily by reading more books.

You don't want to get yourself in the same predicament every day, where you wake up and go to work or school, then come home, and do the same thing again day after day. Most adults call this "the rat race." You don't want to live a very mundane rat race. Find something that you're passionate about and try with all your heart to accomplish that goal.

You must find a way of getting yourself out of the daily routine of that rat race, where you don't enjoy your life situation, by doing something different. Don't expect to be repeating the same day, but expecting different results. Hopefully you start a business or make an investment that will generate you a profit, so that you can have more time freedom to do the things you love.

There are several different ways to make investments. When investing, you are making your money work for you. When working at a steady job, you're working for the money you're receiving. The decisions you make throughout your lifetime are just that: they are choices.

Try to figure out a way to become self-employed, so that you're working on making yourself a profit, and earn yourself a net worth instead of just a salary. When you work for a big company you're making that company a massive profit. Like I said it before, if you can't work hard enough for yourself to accomplish your own dreams, someone will pay you a salary so that you can work on theirs.

CHAPTER 7

CREDIT

How good is your credit score?

A credit score is based on your "credit worthiness." Three companies keep a record of your credit score. These three companies are called Equifax, Experian, and Transunion. These companies collect information about you, whenever it relates to bills, debt, payments, and loans.

If you want to finance a car, the car company checks your credit score. Your credit score is a big indicator of whether that car company can trust you enough to lease you a vehicle. A credit score can determine whether you're a good candidate to be given a loan, and it can also determine what your interest rate will be. The better your credit score, the higher your credit limit might be from a credit card company, and the more opportunities you have to get higher loans, better interest rates, and good prices overall.

You will learn, as you get older, how credit scores can affect you across all areas of life. A credit score can also show derogatory marks—when you have missed payments, for example, or when something might have gone to collections. There is a website called nerdwallet.com that explains all the different types of credit cards available to you. Research and discover which credit card would be best suitable for your interests. I recommend that you look at cards with low fixed APR rates, and also credit cards that have no annual fees. There are also cards that offer rewards points, which offer you money back simply for using that card.

A good credit score can affect you in a positive way, while a bad credit score can hurt you. An example of how a bad credit score can hurt you is when it comes to getting a job: job agencies check to see your credit score, so that they can determine whether you are or are not a responsible person. A bad credit score can also affect your ability to purchase a vehicle, get a mortgage loan, or just a personal loan. You can do certain things to raise your credit score, and to protect yourself against anyone using your identity to mess up your credit score. One of these things is to check your score once a year. There's a website called myfreecreditscore.com, which allows you to see your credit report so that you can dispute anything on it that may not be accurate. I will briefly explain to you below how I established a very good credit score within two years.

First you need to understand that it takes time to raise your credit score, since one thing that the credit reporting agencies look at is the period over which you have had credit. It can be very difficult to establish good credit in the beginning, since most companies don't trust a "clean" credit report. They don't know whether you will default on the payments or not. Credit reporting agencies calculate your credit-worthiness using five different categories.

The first and most important factor is your ability to pay back your credit cards or loans on time. Paying on time makes up 35% of your total score. Another 30% of that score is based on your credit utilization, 15% is on your credit age history, 10% is based on your credit mix, and the final 10% is based on new credit inquiries. I will explain each one individually, so that you can grasp the importance of credit, and how each factor is determined. After I explain to you how each factor contributes to your overall credit score, I will explain how I built up my credit, and what I recommend the best way to build your own credit.

Paying on Time: This first factor is the most important factor in determining your credit score. Paying on time shows a good ability to pay back your future bills. Credit companies see what trade lines you have opened, and how often you are paying them off. A credit line is called a "trade line." The credit companies will determine your score based on whether you make your payments, miss some payments, or are completely delinquent on a trade line. Paying your monthly payments on time guarantees that your paying-on-time factor will always stay at 100%, which is what you want to strive for.

Credit Utilization: The second factor, which is called credit card utilization, means the amount of money you are spending on credit should be less than 30% of the total credit limit. I personally would recommend that you stay below 20% so that your credit worthiness shows you can better handle credit. An example of credit utilization would be having a credit card with a limit of $100. If you're using only $30 of that card, and this is the only card you have, then you have a 30% utilization. You are only utilizing 30% out of the $100 credit card.

Credit Age: The third factor, which is called credit age history, is just the overall time you have had credit. The age history of your credit is only 15% of your overall credit score. If you have more than one type of credit card, or different kinds of credit, then your credit report will show your combined total time and give you an average. The greater time you spend with a credit agency, the better your credit age history will be. It will affect you in a positive way to keep your oldest credit card active on your account. If you ever close your account, it can affect you in a negative way.

Credit Mix: The fourth factor comprises only 10% of your overall credit score. This category is called your credit mix. Your credit mix is exactly what it sounds like—it is a mixture of all the types of credit you may have. An example of someone's credit mix might be a car loan, mortgage loan, bank loan, school loan, and a few credit cards. A person with that variety of credit mix might be scored highly, as long as their credit card utilization is low, and they are making their monthly payments on time every month.

Credit Card Inquiries: The final factor that makes up another 10% of your score is your credit card inquiries. Each time you are interested in applying for a credit card, or a loan from the bank, a new car, or whatever you're trying to do that needs financing, you will have to get your credit report "pulled." You can either have a soft inquiry or a hard inquiry. A soft inquiry is when your entire credit report is not pulled by an agency, and this kind of inquiry does not affect your credit score. A hard inquiry is when a lender checks to see all the details of your credit worthiness, and you will see a change in your credit score. You will either see a small change, or a big change, depending on how that inquiry affects your five factors. The more inquires that a person has within a short period, the more lenders will consider you a high risk, since you're "credit hungry." You're showing creditors that you are in need of credit. The key to keeping your utilization down is to not try and get multiple credit cards all at once. Like I first mentioned when talking about credit, it takes time for you to build up a good credit score, so you shouldn't rush to build your credit fast.

There are credit repair companies that promise to help you build your credit fast, but remember that anything that sounds too good to be true usually is. Below, I will explain the different methods you can use to increase your credit score. I will also teach you one trick that isn't discussed often when it comes to credit. There are multiple ways to increase your credit, but I will explain here what worked for me.

How to build your credit

The first way you can build you credit is most suitable for someone without a good chance of getting credit, for whatever reason. In this case, a bank will issue you something called a "secured credit card." A secured credit card is exactly that. The bank will use your own money to give you a credit card, under the promise that you will pay it back. If you cannot pay back the amount you use on the card, the bank will simply keep the money you used in the first place to secure that card. The bank understands that you're a high-risk person. The limit on that secured card will be the exact amount of money that they will keep from your account.

Another way for you to slowly increase your credit score is for you to take out a small loan from a loan company. Start with a simple loan of $100. The loan company will loan you the money, with interest. The interest rate a loan company offers is usually high. For a $100 loan, you will likely pay them back $140. This means that the loan company will lend you $100, and you pay an extra $40 in return for being able to borrow that money. The great thing about a loan company is that they will report your loan to the credit agencies, allowing you to slowly build up credit.

You can also build your credit by having someone who will co-sign for you. For example, if you want to buy a car, but you don't have good credit, your mother, father, or a friend can co-sign for the loan with you. This allows both people to be responsible for the payments due on the car. The person who has already established credit is essentially vouching for the person without credit. In this scenario, both parties make sure the loan gets paid back.

These are three easy ways you can build your credit. There are lots of other ways to build your credit, so whatever way you want to try, just start now. It's never too late to build your credit.

Once you have established a good credit history, I have some further advice for building up your credit quickly and easily. To do this, I recommend that you get a card from a bank, ideally a big bank such as Chase, which has multiple cards that you can use to your advantage.

I started with the Chase Freedom Card, for which I was initially given a $5,000 credit limit. After six months of having the Freedom Card and paying it back on time, I requested a credit limit increase. A credit limit increase is not always guaranteed, but it's worth trying. I was given a $3,000 increase.

After another six months of having the card, I requested another increase, in which I was again given the same increase of

$3,000 dollars. Within one year I went from $5,000 to $11,000. I then applied for a different credit card with Chase, called the Freedom Unlimited, for which I was given a $5,000 limit. I then called customer service to see if I would be able to transfer my old limit from my Freedom card to my new Freedom Unlimited card, which they allowed me to.

The only stipulation was that I would have to keep $1,000 on my unlimited card. I transferred $10,000 and started with $15,000 in my Freedom Unlimited card, with 0% interest for the next 15 months. Every six months, I requested a limit increase on both cards. I was given a $5,000 increase on both cards, and I then transferred the limit to one card.

This is how, in a matter of two years, I went from a $5,000 limit on one card to a $25,000 limit on a new card, with 18 months of no interest. Learn how to play with your own credit limits. Remember that having a high limit with a low utilization rate shows that you know how to manage your credit score well.

After the promotion ran out, I applied for another card. I then applied for the Chase Slate Card, for which I was given a $15,000 limit to begin with. I requested a limit increase again on both my Freedom and Freedom Unlimited, and was given a $5,000 increase on each card. I then transferred this $23,000 to my $13,000 Slate Card limit, meaning that I started my Slate Card with $46,000 limit with 0% interest for the next 15 months. I took the knowledge that

I learned about credit, and used it to my advantage. Understanding how credit works is important. The great thing was that the Chase Slate Card had a promotion of balance transfer, so I transferred my higher-interest cards to the credit card that offered 0% interest for 15 months.

The final thing I will mention about credit is called "piggybacking." This is a method by which you piggyback on another person's trade line.

Let me give you an example of what I mean. Let's say a person has absolutely no credit, but knows someone like myself who has excellent credit. I can add that person with no good credit as an authorized user on my $46,000-limit cards. By doing this, that person just became credit-worthy, since the records will show that he or she has a credit card with a $46,000 limit.

There are various way that people can piggyback to get ahead with their credit scores. If you need more information, there are books that specifically talk about credit. I hope I have educated you enough that you will now strive to reach an excellent credit level. Paying off all your payments on time is a very important obligation.

Now that we have spoken about credit, let's play a quick game. I will give you different scenarios, and you must select the right answer.

Who will have the worst credit deal?

Option A: There is a man with a $100,000 loan at 4% interest. He is on a 30-year term. His monthly payment will be $800 a month.

Option B: There is a woman with a $100,000 loan for a house at 8% interest. She is on a 30-year term. Her monthly payments are $1,600 a month.

Option C: A man purchased a $200,000 home with a 50% down payment, an interest rate of 4%, and he is on a 15-year loan with a monthly payment of $1,600 a month.

Who will pay the most interest at the end of their term?

Option A will pay $188,000 of interest over 30 years.

Option B will pay $576,000 of interest over 30 years.

Option C will pay $188,000 of interest over 15 years.

Option B will pay the most.

These numbers are a representation of what credit looks like. In life you will eventually have to deal with credit, so you might as well try to get the best interest rates and research what it takes to get the best credit scores possible. Hopefully these tricks of the trade I have shared with you will help you to increase your credit score.

Obligations

Everyone has different obligations in life to fulfill. An obligation is a duty or a commitment that a person must perform. An example of an obligation is when a child is going to school. That child's obligation is to do the homework, get good grades, and graduate from high school so that they get a career.

A college student's obligation is to take the proper courses they need to get their degree. An adult's obligation might be to become the provider of a household and pay the bills. As a person grows older, their obligations change. A child's obligations are a lot different from the obligations of an adult with children.

The sooner you understand that you have obligations in life, the better you will become at accomplishing your obligations. It doesn't matter at what age you are when you understand that you have an obligation. The only thing that matters is that you fulfil those obligations.

Firstly, you need to understand that everyone has a distinct obligation they must fulfill. As I have discussed, a child's obligations might differ from an adult's. A child's obligation might consist of being respectful towards adults, and to continue to increase their learning abilities by going to school. Some children might be held to a higher expectation by an adult, such as getting straight A's at school. Children may also have obligations at home, such as taking the garbage out, or making sure that certain chores are being take care of. Every child has different obligations because everyone is raised differently.

A high school teacher has the obligation to make sure that their students comprehend the subject being taught to them. Every teacher has a different obligation towards their students, but their main obligation is to make their students understand the material being taught to them so that they can pass their exit-level exams. Sports educators have a different type of obligation towards their students. A football coach must teach their students teamwork, and to function better by working as a team. Teamwork shows the students how important it is to work together to accomplish more.

An employee's obligation is to get to work on time, in order not to get fired. An employee must also follow certain rules and regulations, depending on the job, if they are to excel and succeed in the job. Being punctual and doing their job is important. You must give 110% whenever you do something. An employer's job is to make sure that the employees are following the rules in order not to get fired.

Anyone with a career or job must be skilled enough for the tasks they must perform. Would you want someone to perform surgery on you if they have no experience? You must be able to get the experience required for you to do your job correctly.

We all have different obligations we need to abide by to get through life. You must make a clear distinction about your obligations, and how you can fulfil them. It would not be a smart choice to quit your job when bills still need to be paid. Think logically about all the decisions you make in life.

CHAPTER 8
TAKE ACTION

Be productive!

Firstly, you must understand that there will always be something you can learn from someone else. Everyone thinks differently, so learn to benefit from the thinking patterns of others. Make sure that the person you're trying to emulate is someone who has succeeded, or is on his or her way to success. You must make sure that you get your information from the right people.

You must educate yourself by reading as much informative information. Don't procrastinate and do nothing productive throughout the day. Boredom is only a state of mind. You need to realize that the people who are never bored are the ones who create things. These people make things happen.

Are you a person who always wants to do more? Time is money for those with a plan. Don't just have a plan—work every day towards accomplishing it.

Ask yourself, **"How productive am I, and can I increase my level or productivity?"**

_____

_____

_____

_____

Example: Yes, I am a productive person! I value my time tremendously. There's never enough time for me to do everything I want to do in one full day.

Remember that there will always be something productive and interesting to learn about, so don't make the excuse that there is nothing to do. Those who use their time wisely are the ones who will succeed, while those who wait until tomorrow never accomplish anything.

The present is when you should put your plans to action. Living in America gives you the advantage of having a free enterprise economy. You must take advantage of what life offers. Each day that you're alive, try to make the most of it.

Your life's purpose is what you want it to be. You must be in charge of your future. Take control of your life by doing what is right. Don't take life for granted. Some of the simplest things in life are taken for granted, like being able to breathe, see, talk, hear, and smell. Not everyone is lucky enough to be born with all five of his or her senses working properly.

When I was younger, I once complained about not having the shoes I wanted, until I saw a person with their legs amputated. You must be grateful for everything that you have been blessed with. How can you explain to a blind person that has never seen in their life how beautiful the sky looks?

Too often, Americans take a lot of things for granted. You need to realize that not everyone is privileged enough to have a house, car, or running hot water. Some children in other countries die from starvation, while people in the United States die from overeating. Not all countries have access to clean running water. Usually the rich people in impoverished countries are the only ones that can take showers daily.

Here in America, education is given to the public for free. You must take advantage of this and learn as much as you can. Get yourself access to an unlimited amount of information by signing up for a library card. You can also read a lot of information on the Internet. Always continue your education, even if you're not going to school.

Be grateful that you are learning in a country with free food in public schools. Not all countries are lucky enough to be treated like Americans. This is why so many people get killed trying to get into America. This is the land of the free and the home of the brave. You must use your freedom by making the most out of it. Create a business and try to make the most out of your life. Don't always be waiting until the next day to accomplish something. The next day is already, **today**!

Jump

We live in a generation which is always procrastinating, putting off going things until tomorrow or the following day. Some of us live life as if we are going to live forever. The greatest advice I was ever given was from an older gentleman. I asked him if he could go back in time and give himself advice, what that advice would be. The advice he would give to his younger self was, "jump." I didn't understand that concept at first, until he explained it to me in more detail.

He told me: in life you're given two choices. The first choice is to accept life the way it is, and be content to live life in a rat race where you have a daily routine that doesn't change. This first choice is the choice that many of us make. We live life and take it for what it is. This first choice is not the one we thought we would be living, but most of us end up living it.

The second option, this man told me, was the option to jump. Now, he was not literally talking about jumping, but he was trying to explain how we come across many situations in life where we are at a crossroads. We want to follow our dreams and conquer our goals in life. But doubt, fear, and worry get into our minds. We doubt that we are not good enough to accomplish our dreams, or we might hear someone tell us we aren't good enough to do something we love in life and we learn to accept that message. The man said, "You must jump," and take a leap of faith and try your hardest to follow your dreams and accomplish your goals.

He mentioned that we should live each day as if it is our last. You don't know when you are going to die. We all have a clock over our heads, and each day we live that clock ticks away. We don't know when our last day here on Earth might be, so we must take advantage of our life and do something positive each day.

If you knew that today was your last day to be alive, would you be doing what you do daily? This is something that you must figure out for yourself. Tomorrow is never promised to any of us. We don't know when our time to die might arrive.

Just because you don't know when it's your time to die doesn't mean that you can't prepare for the future. You must save your money, or invest, and not just live life carelessly spending your money, without thinking of the future. To jump means that you should live your life with purpose, and take the risk, take the change, be different, be unique. Work each day with purpose.

In 100 years' time, you won't be remembered for the things you didn't do in your life, but for the things you *did*. Leave behind a legacy—a legacy of how you want to be remembered. Albert Einstein will forever be remembered for his ability to solve a mathematical equation that changed the world. Leonardo da Vinci will forever be remembered because of his ability to paint the way he did.

Don't do the same things daily and expect to get different results. Continually push your boundaries and limits and find ways to grow. You must teach yourself by gaining as much knowledge as possible across different areas in life, and by learning to go the extra mile by becoming a producer.

Ask yourself, **"If I knew I was going to die tomorrow, would I still be living the life I live?"**

_____

_____

_____

_____

Producers and consumers!

Life is not all about becoming successful overnight. You need to understand that success takes time. You can't be born a successful person—you must *earn* your success. You must be willing to go the extra mile to accomplish any task. Like I've said before, wake up earlier, go to sleep later to work on becoming successful.

Competitive Olympic athletes train every day for years on end in order to be labeled the best. When you see them on TV, they may make what they do look effortless, but you don't see the hard work and stress they endured to get to the level of competition they are at. They have worked extremely hard at being the best.

People rarely see the hard work and sacrifice that many successful people have endured. Great salesmen have had lots of doors shut in their faces, but they persisted in selling. You must have the same enthusiasm for becoming successful. You must use your time to figure out a way for you to succeed.

Take a chance at the risk of failure. There can't be a winner without having a loser. Make the choice to become a winner. A person that has never failed has never tried. Always try to be great in whatever you do.

You must realize that most people who make large fortunes are producers. Every single human on this earth is a consumer. We go to the store and buy the necessities we need to survive, such as the food we eat, the clothes we wear, or the toothpaste we use. Consumers keep the economy balanced. Consumers help the market by creating employment opportunities. By producing a product, you're creating a market. Think about all people you know who are producers.

To get past poverty you must figure out how to become a producer instead of just a consumer. It's all about supply and demand. If there is huge demand for a product, people will pay for that product, simply because the demand is there. A product like oil, however, is called a "monopoly." Whatever price the people who control the oil set, that is the price that ordinary average Americans must pay. You need gas to transport yourself to work, so it basically becomes a need.

Most successful people in this world are producers. Producers create a product which people need, and which there is a demand for. They make the product and sell it. Think about some of the most successful producers you know. These people produce clothing, food, games, inventions, apps, businesses that sell a product or service.

You must figure out how to create something that will benefit future generations. Many successful media moguls are entrepreneurs. They become successful and learn to promote cologne, clothing, and even the endorsement deals they have made with large corporations. Anybody can become famous with the internet. Teenager's are making very popular social media accounts where they have a massive influence on the younger demographics. The younger generation is a generation of technology. They can use that social influence to sell themselves as a brand, or to sell a product or service. Use social media to your advantage and try to create a massive audience.

Famous media moguls take advantage of being famous, so that they can advertise a product and get lots of people interested with that product. Famous people create a demand among consumers, because of their popularity. A famous talk show host like Oprah can recommend any book, and it becomes an instant best-seller automatically. It doesn't matter what kind of book it is. It's all about advertising, marketing, and supply and demand.

You must be figure out a way to create a product. By creating product, you're allowing yourself to make a certain profit. You are the only one who will know the percentage you're making. It all depends on the products you are thinking about creating. Producing something allows you to have consumers for that product. A book is one example of a product.

How can I become a producer?

_____

_____

_____

_____

Example: By writing a book, I'm becoming a producer.

Game: will you become a millionaire?

Let's play a game. Hopefully throughout this book, you have been writing down your answers with each question I've asked. The reason I ask you to write down answers to my questions, is so you can have a better understanding of who you are as a person, and what your future will look like. Each question that I have written, was written with the intentions for you to get value out of it.

Write down in the space below what you would do if someone were to hypothetically give you one million dollars for no apparent reason. I want you to write down every material thing you would want to purchase, including the cars you'd want to buy with this imaginary money, the house, and any other luxury items you can think of. Be specific with the money and the amount that those items cost. You can include anything you want. Your choices are limited to the million-dollar budget you have been given. Remember that you must put down the price for every item you have written down. Make sure to spend all of the million dollars.

What will I do with one million dollars?

_____

_____

_____

_____

Now I want you to write down where you see yourself five years after you were given this imaginary money. Think about whether you wasted the money without investing, or whether you invested this imaginary money in ways that will make your money multiply?

Where do I see myself 5 years after getting this one million dollars?

_____

_____

_____

_____

If you made more money than the million dollars given to you, then you figured out a way for you to budget what you're spending and invested it in something profitable. If you spent the money on a big house, extravagant cars, and materialistic items, then you still haven't figured out on how to invest. Most people want to purchase high-priced items, and not invest. You need to learn that the only way to make your money last is to manage it well by investing it.

If you were the type of person that wanted to purchase those extravagant items without investing any of your money, then how would you be able to get that money to begin with? Also, how would you be able to manage those luxury items? You must have an income if you want to continue living an extravagant lifestyle.

Knowing how to budget is essential. Now I want you to write down how you could get that imaginary million dollars in real life. Think of a business plan that would allow you to make that money. Some people will automatically think of either a criminal way of obtaining the money, such as robbing a bank, while others will just hope and pray that with some luck they might win the lottery.

Which type of person are you? In reality, neither way would do you any good. The best way for you to get what you want is to work hard for your money. The harder you work, the luckier you'll get. You must apply your talents and pursue your dreams by figuring out a way to achieve them. Even in most high-paying jobs, it will take years to finally earn a million dollars. You can't expect to earn a lot of money by being lazy. You must make a plan and stick to it. Don't just live day by day with no plan.

Life is what you make of it. You are the only one capable of doing the things that you've always wanted to do. In life you will always have to face obstacles, but always remember the little train that could. Always be thinking in your head, "I KNOW I CAN, I KNOW I CAN!"

I have changed the words on purpose, from "I think," to "I know!" A little self-motivation can lead to enduring success in your life. Always be thinking of success and not failure. You must have the conscious mindset that you can accomplish any task life has given you. Your thoughts control your actions, so think of success! You must envision success in your mind and know that you're capable of anything.

Now let's set aside this unrealistic game and talk about reality. Reality isn't a game, and shouldn't be discussed that way. I put it in perspective as a game, to help you realize that you may actually have to deal with numbers realistically. I want you to figure out at what age you plan on moving out of your house and into your own home? There is a lot of responsibility involved in moving out and living on your own. Think about your situation. Figure out what you're doing, and what you want to accomplish in life. Think of all your goals and aspirations. Focus and concentrate on how you will try to reach your goals.

Key ingredients for success

Most people make the mistake of thinking that there is only one way to become successful. This is not true. You have been told a lie. Don't believe that there is only one key secret to becoming successful. Success doesn't have a shortcut or a secret sauce or a single magical ingredient. Success takes time, and involves multiple factors. I have studied a wide variety of successful entrepreneurs from all walks of life and have learned they all have key traits for becoming successful.

These key traits are hard work, dedication, determination, passion, drive, and the willingness to continually learn and grow and develop. These successful people are continuous learners. They don't stop learning right after school. They continue to teach themselves whatever they want to learn.

Successful people focus on personal growth, to become better than before. These people are the dream chasers. Successful people have goals in life they want to accomplish. They have the vision to significantly change their lives. They not only have goals, but they act on their goals. They work hard day in and day out to get their goals accomplished. They wake up earlier, go to sleep later, have mentors they look up to, read daily, and always look for ways to grow in life.

TAKE ACTION

I hope I have inspired you find your purpose. Remember that success is not a destination but a journey. In life you can either focus or flounder. Focus on the things that make you happy. Work harder than your competition and people will see you working. Let your success make noise. Become so important that people pay you for your time. Become so successful that you won't need to introduce yourself, that your signature will be called an autograph. You will become great in whatever you put your mind to. Work hard so your future self can look back at the past and see how much you have grown. Remember that the key to success is to start now.

Reality = TAKE ACTION!

You must alter your conscious mind to create new ideas, write down the thoughts that you're thinking, and apply the knowledge I have shared here. I have done extensive research to uncover the true reason for why some people succeed, while others fail. Understand the information you have read here and apply it. Make sure that all your thoughts lead to a positive happy healthy life, and destroy the habit of procrastination.

Know that we are all just spiritual beings living through a human experience. So learn to clear your mind of the daily distractions of the world and concentrate on the more important issues in life. Do as much as you can in an entire day.

We are all human, so try to leave behind a legacy. Death is inevitable. Humans are fallible, so be prepared to make mistakes in life. Learn not only from your own mistakes, but also from the mistakes of others. Be pleased with life, for life is a precious story, and every day is a new chapter.

Throughout this book I have covered a wide variety of different topics, which ranged from goals, success, ambition, vision, dreams, money, positive mentality, career, jobs, lifestyle, time, time management, independence, becoming a provider, special talents, skills, value, assets, liabilities, investments, businesses, reality, not giving up, personal growth, credit score, and so much more valuable information.

The things which I have covered here comprise all that it takes to become successful. Success is a state of mind. We all have a different interpretation of what success means to us. Reaching a level of success means reaching a level of happiness. The end result, in whatever you do in life, is to be happy.

I hope that my book has inspired you to do something positive with your life. Shoot for the moon, because even if you miss, you'll still end up amongst the stars. Never give up and always try hard. I wish you the best of luck and happiness with your adventure towards success. Succeeding is not the end of the journey, but the beginning. Every day you should find new meaning in the greatest adventure of all, known as life.

Treat life as if it were a **BOOK**. Every day is a new page, and every encounter with a person is a new paragraph. Compile your book of "life" using the beauty of what life has to offer. Don't be afraid to explore something new. Life is all about exploration, growth and discovery.

Discover the past if you want to predict the future, but always be willing to explore the future to predict the present. Life will give what you ask for. If you ask for a life of riches, you shall have your life of riches, but don't expect it to come knocking at your front door. You must find out which door to open.

I have now given you the **KEY** to finding your own type of **"SUCCESS!"** It is now up to you to **TAKE ACTION**!

"To be great, is to be misunderstood."

– Ralph Waldo Emerson

VISIT MY SOCIAL MEDIA PLATFORMS

Feel Free to Add me on all of my social media platforms.

Snapchat: RgVAuthor

Facebook: RgVAuthor:

https://www.facebook.com/RgVAuthor/

Instagram: RgVAuthor:

https://www.instagram.com/rgvauthor/

Twitter: RgVAuthor1

https://twitter.com/RgVAuthor1

Pinterest: RgVAuthor

https://www.pinterest.com/RgVAuthor/pins/

YouTube: RgVAuthor

https://www.youtube.com/channel/UC5lQA5AzA_RIT39ectHEk
1w?disable_polymer=true

If you want to personally reach out to me, send me an e-mail.

Email= RGVAUTHOR@GMAIL.COM